SOME THOUGHTS ON HITLER

AND OTHER ESSAYS

by

IRMIN VINSON

EDITED BY GREG JOHNSON

FOREWORD BY KEVIN MACDONALD

Counter-Currents Publishing Ltd.
San Francisco
2012

Copyright © 2012 by Counter-Currents Publishing Ltd.
All rights reserved

Cover image:
Courtesy of The Savitri Devi Archive
http://www.savitridevi.org/

Cover design:
Kevin I. Slaughter

Published in the United States by
COUNTER-CURRENTS PUBLISHING LTD.
P.O. Box 22638
San Francisco, CA 94122
USA
http://www.counter-currents.com/

Hardcover ISBN: 978-1-935965-25-1

Paperback ISBN: 978-1-935965-26-8

E-book ISBN: 978-1-935965-27-5

Library of Congress Cataloguing-in-Publication Data:

Vinson, Irmin, 1969–
  Some thoughts on Hitler and other essays / by Irmin Vinson ; edited by Greg Johnson ; foreword by Kevin Macdonald.
      p. cm.
  Includes bibliographical references and index.
  ISBN 978-1-935965-25-1 (hardcover : alk. paper) -- ISBN 978-1-935965-26-8 (pbk. : alk. paper)
  1. National socialism. 2. Ethnicity. 3. Caucasian race. 4. Jews--Germany--History--1933-1945. 5. Holocaust, Jewish (1939-1945)--Germany. 6. Hitler, Adolf, 1889-1945--Political and social views. I. Johnson, Greg, 1971- II. Title.

DD253.V56 2011
305.8--dc23

Contents

Editor's Note by Greg Johnson ♦ v

Foreword by Kevin MacDonald ♦ vii

White Racial Nationalism
1. Some Thoughts on Hitler ♦ 1
2. Racial Nationalism and the Aryans ♦ 7

The Jewish Question
3. Holocaust Commemoration ♦ 14
4. Remembering the Holocaust ♦ 64
5. Spielberg and the Eleven Million ♦ 90
6. The Mufti and Martin Hohmann ♦ 99
7. The Holocaust as Weapon ♦ 104
8. *The Patriot*: Reviewing a Review ♦ 110
9. Gibson, Jesus, and the Jews ♦ 121
10. Jesus and the ADL ♦ 125
11. Jewish Hypocrisy and the One-State Solution ♦ 129
12. Ruling the World by Proxy ♦ 135

The Muslim Question
13. Jews, Islam, and Orientalism ♦ 139
14. Abrogated Verses in the Koran ♦ 147
15. The Lessons of Madrid ♦ 152

White Ethnomasochism
16. Wagner and Multiracialism ♦ 156
17. Some Remarks on "Racism" ♦ 161
18. Amy Biehl: A White Liberal on the Dark Continent ♦ 164
19. Jane Elliott and Diversity Training ♦ 174

"Yield to all and you will soon have nothing to yield." — Aesop

Editor's Note

Irmin Vinson is the pen name of a thought criminal who wishes to remain as mysterious as Homer or Shakespeare. I know him only from his work. This collection of his essays is drawn from his website Irminsul's Racial Nationalist Library (http://library.flawlesslogic.com/) as well as the now defunct *National Vanguard* webzine.

The Racial Nationalist Library first went online in 1999. I discovered it sometime in 2000, and it played an important role in my education as a White Nationalist. It was not a quick journey. There was no sudden and dramatic "conversion" experience. Instead, it was a long process of reading and discussion (with two friends) that began in January of 1999 and has never really stopped. I am an intellectual, after all. I had to square White Nationalism with my reason, my conscience, and my general aesthetic sensibility. It had to be true, good, and beautiful. I never set foot in a public gathering until I attended a lecture by David Irving on Labor Day of 2000.

Part of my hesitation to take my journey into the real world was the establishment's carefully crafted image of White Nationalists as an unsavory collection of cranks and kooks. I knew this was not entirely true, of course, because I had ample written evidence to the contrary (Kevin MacDonald's *The Culture of Critique*, for instance). But, unfortunately, much of what I encountered online tended to confirm the negative stereotypes.

This is why I found the Racial Nationalist Library so impressive. Everything about the site—from its elegant design and well-chosen illustrations to its highbrow but hard-hitting content—quieted my qualms, allowing me to fully open my mind to the assembled texts, which methodically demonstrated that White Nationalism is a worldview consistent with reason, morality, and good taste. White Nationalism is not marginal by nature. Instead, it is the legitimate heir—and the only possible continuation—of the best of the Western intellectual and political tradition. White Nationalism has merely been marginalized and stigmatized by our Jewish-dominated political and intellectual establishment, which has instituted the truly aberrant reign of multiculturalism to slowly exterminate our race.

The Racial Nationalist Library was one of the primary inspirations for the Counter-Currents/*North American New Right* webzine. Thus it was only natural to reprint its articles from time to time, to bring them to new audiences. On April 20, 2011, we reprinted Irmin's "Some Thoughts on Hitler." It became wildly popular and is by far the most widely-read article on our site. Apparently, Irmin's ability to express radically un-PC ideas with calm, clarity, and careful logic has struck a chord. Hence the decision to assemble this collection in search of still wider audiences.

I want to thank Irmin Vinson for his permission to publish this collection and his help in assembling and editing it. Special thanks are due Kevin MacDonald for his Foreword. I also wish to thank Matthew Peters for his meticulous proofreading, Kevin Slaughter for designing the cover, Michael Polignano for preparing the manuscript for the Library of Congress cataloguing process, the Savitri Devi Archive for permission to use the cover photograph,[1] and Kerry Bolton and Mark Weber for their publicity blurbs.

Greg Johnson
San Francisco, November 27, 2011

---

[1] Savitri Devi, *Long-Whiskers and the Two-Legged Goddess* (Calcutta: Savitri Devi Mukherji, 1965), 16.

Foreword

Kevin MacDonald

Irmin Vinson is a very talented writer who deserves a wide audience. This is an excellent collection of essays by someone who has thought long and hard about the threats to our people and our culture.

As Mr. Vinson notes in the title essay, National Socialism was indeed an attempt to secure the ethnic interests of the German people, just as Judaism and Israel are attempts to secure the ethnic interests of Jews. It is certainly not necessary to defend all aspects of National Socialism in order to defend the idea that Whites have legitimate ethnic interests, as much as our enemies try to link White identity with National Socialism. As he notes, the opposite of National Socialism is globalism and multiculturalism—an ideal that Jews advocate only in the Diaspora in the West while vigorously opposing it as a model for Israel.

We should not shrink from these comparisons, especially in the light of modern evidence clearly showing the biological roots of race. Races are indeed extended families with an interest in long term survival. There are also well-documented race differences in traits critical for the success of complex contemporary societies. These race differences are on display in this collection, particularly in Vinson's essay on Africa where he notes Black inability to create productive economies or any semblance of democratic government.

These essays are invariably well thought out and well-grounded in empirical data. His essay on the Indo-Europeans quite rightly emphasizes the contribution of the primordial peoples of Europe prior to the Indo-

European invasions of the 4th millennium B.C. Whereas the other areas dominated by Indo-Europeans quickly reverted to the collectivist cultural tendencies typical of the rest of the world, only Europe produced a distinctive culture of individualism with all that that entails in terms of political culture: tendencies that ultimately resulted in individual rights against the state and republican political cultures with deep roots in Western history going back to the ancient world. Any adequate theory of Western uniqueness must include the influence of the primordial cultures of Europe that existed prior to the Indo-European invasions.

Vinson's comments on the Holocaust emphasize the image of the Holocaust as a creation of Jewish intellectuals with access to the media and as an instrument of Jewish political power not only in defense of Israel but as a weapon against White interests. Indeed, the Holocaust is the ultimate moral justification for multiculturalism and massive non-White immigration. As he writes "If the Holocaust is ... the Jewish collective memory of World War II, then we who are not Jews are in effect thinking about our past with someone else's memory, seeing both the past and its implications for the present through Jewish eyes rather than through our own."

I was unaware of Arthur Miller's novel *Focus*, published in 1945. It is quite clearly a classic work of Jewish ethnic activism by someone who was well-connected to the halls of literary power and therefore able to influence popular opinion. The book is a good example of Jewish hostility toward the people and culture of the West. Its subtext is the Jewish alliance with non-Whites that would become the Jewish postwar strategy, apparent, for example, of the powerful Jewish support for Black interests. But its main importance is an early version of the Holocaust as a tool of Jewish ethnic interests. Miller "took it upon himself to teach an early version of what would eventually become the most insidious of the Jewish Holocaust's numerous lessons, namely that pathological ('nazi') hatreds lurk behind the West's superficially civilized exterior." It is an image that continues to reverberate throughout the West. The war against National Socialism is now depicted as a huge moral lapse of the West for failing to do enough to help the Jews. German concentration camps were transformed into symbols of "generalized White guilt"—symbols of the "vast moral failure" of Western civilization. It is quite accurate to state that Holocaust scholarship is essentially "an aggressive scrounging for sources of [Jewish] racial grievance."

The Holocaust as weapon against the West represents a departure from the World War II rhetoric of good democracies against evil fascism:

> The war's aftermath offered a didactic opportunity to define anti-Semitism as incompatible with the West's highest ideals, which Allied soldiers had supposedly shed their blood defending. With Hitler's defeat the enemies of the Jews were placed outside our Civilization, which should have encouraged Jews to curtail their frequent efforts to subvert it.
>
> The Jewish group decision to shape their Holocaust memory into an indictment of Western "anti-Semitism" and "racism"—our "pathology"—was a calculated repudiation of post-war triumphalism. The Jewish Holocaust, as it emerged from the burgeoning identity politics of the 1960s, blurred and even effaced what had formerly been a clear distinction between *them* and *us*, cruel dictatorships and civilized democracies, and it set Jewry apart from both.

An overarching theme here is the falsification of history in the service of Jewish ethnic interests by Jews with access to the media. Vinson has a priceless review of Steven Spielberg's TV miniseries, *Band of Brothers*, exposing its intellectual gymnastics in the service of Jewish ethnic interests. Another essay comments on the historical omissions apparent in the hostile review of the movie *Patriot* by a Jewish reviewer, Jonathan Foreman: omitting crucial details of a World War II German massacre in the service of indicting the West, not to mention Foreman's antipathy for well-functioning White families and Aryan-looking heroes depicted as defending their people. The essay on Mel Gibson capitulating to Jewish pressure to change a scene in *The Passion of the Christ* (a scene based on the Bible), in which a Jewish mob calls for the crucifixion of Jesus, makes a larger point about Jewish power in America. Not only did Jews manage to intimidate Gibson, they did so despite the fact that the Talmud clearly states that Jesus was executed by a proper rabbinical court for idolatry.

History is whatever Jewish activists in the media (and the academic world) want to make of it. History is what is good for the Jews.

This falsification in the service of Jewish ethnic goals is also apparent in the essay titled "Jews, Islam, and Orientalism" where "Jewish scholarship concealed its anti-European aggression in the learned pages of sympathetic studies of Islam." The result has been to sanitize Islam as part of a campaign to admit millions of Muslims into Europe and ultimately to displace the peoples and culture of the West. Amazingly, this campaign coincides with neoconservative Jews routinely vilifying militant Islam in the interests of defending Israel against its Middle Eastern enemies. Once again, Jewish activists are able to have their cake and eat it too, in this case representing Muslim immigrants to the West as benign assimilators who do not threaten Western identity while promoting attempts to rearrange the politics of the Middle East in the interests of Israel.

Another form of falsification occurs with Richard Wagner who produced powerful music that brought to life the ethnonationalist mythology of the German people. Wagner's music is so powerful that it cannot be ignored, resulting in a strategy where his "threatening art must therefore be aggressively reproduced in misshapen travesties of his original vision." As Vinson notes, all of this rewriting of the past is motivated by fear that the anti-White multiracialist message is inherently weak and unappealing, so that it must constantly be propped up with wall-to-wall propaganda that reaches into every nook and cranny of the cultural landscape, even 19th-century opera:

> Despite wielding all this power, multiracialists know that most Whites have not yet embraced their moral system. Any suggestion that there are legitimate alternatives becomes a source of fearful anxiety. Multiracialists try to prevent their opponents from speaking because they believe that most Whites would want to listen, and thus they fear anything, even old operas by a dead heretic, that challenges their totalitarian ideology.

The emperor has no clothes, requiring an intensive, never-ending effort to make it seem like he's actually very well-dressed.

Finally, I couldn't agree more that "we should never tire of identifying Jewish hypocrisy on racial issues and never fear repetition." A major source of the power of the mainstream media is that it endlessly repeats its anti-White propaganda. The Anti-Defamation League and other Jewish organizations insist on Israel as a Jewish ethnostate and resolutely oppose any sense that governments should pursue the interests of their European-descended majorities. It is perhaps the most glaring hypocrisy imaginable. However, a measure of Jewish power is that Jewish activists routinely engage in this hypocrisy without any fear of being mentioned by mainstream politicians or non-Jews in the media. Both groups are well aware of the calamitous consequences for their careers that would ensue should they violate the taboo about discussing Jewish influence. Although cracks are beginning to appear, mainly as a result of the rise of the Internet, the fact is that Jews have managed to completely control the discourse about Jewish issues, multiculturalism, and the benefits of racial and ethnic diversity with no fear that their double standards, hypocrisy, or falsifications of history will be noticed in the aboveground popular or academic media. It's really an awesome display of Jewish power.

We desperately need to oppose this power. Irmin Vinson is a sophisticated thinker and eloquent writer about all of the issues at the heart of the dispossession of Whites. I highly recommend this collection of his essays.

November 21, 2011

KEVIN MACDONALD, Professor of Psychology at California State University—Long Beach, is the author of *A People That Shall Dwell Alone: Judaism as a Group Evolutionary Strategy* (1994), *Separation and Its Discontents: Toward an Evolutionary Theory of Anti-Semitism* (1998), and *The Culture of Critique: An Evolutionary Analysis of Jewish Involvement in Twentieth-Century Intellectual and Political Movements* (1998), as well as *Cultural Insurrections: Essays on Western Civilization, Jewish Influence, and Anti-Semitism* (2007). He is the editor of *The Occidental Quarterly* and *The Occidental Observer* (http://www.theoccidentalobserver.net).

Some Thoughts on Hitler

"Hitler" as Multiracialist Propaganda

The argument advanced by some racial nationalists that any defense of Adolf Hitler, in light of the hostility and even revulsion that his name now evokes, risks alienating mainstream Whites is plausible on its surface and should receive a respectful hearing. But it is still on balance mistaken.

Although most nationalists in the United States and even in Germany do not consider themselves national socialists, multiracialists and anti-White Jewish advocacy groups call each and every one of us a "nazi." It is an undeniable fact that in our contemporary political climate *any* white nationalism, as recent events in the Balkans amply demonstrate, will be labeled Hitlerian and will summon, in breathless media presentations, "the specter of the Holocaust" and anguished fears that "it" might just happen again, if the *goyim* get too restless. That, after all, is the central lesson taught by the countless Holocaust museums sprouting up, like noxious toadstools, throughout most of the West: that White racial consciousness is literally lethal and must therefore be actively combated, a lesson which we have now enshrined, in deference to Jewry, at the Holocaust Museum in Washington, a national memorial to our White wickedness.

We are thus obliged, like it or not, to live under Hitler's shadow. Our enemies have ensured that any expression of White racial consciousness, however innocuous, will be officially pronounced hatefully Hitlerian and "nazi," whether we admire Hitler or despise him. It is therefore incumbent on us, as a simple matter of self-defense, to arrive at a balanced view of Hitler and the movement he founded.

Anyone who doubts all this should recall the abuse that Pat Buchanan received at the hands of the controlled media and the organized Jewish community during his campaigns for the Republican nomination. Buchanan is not, by any stretch of the imagination, a national socialist, nor even a conscious racialist. He is, instead, a traditional Christian conservative, with all the virtues and liabilities that entails. But he was persistently labeled a "nazi" nevertheless. His 1992 speech at the Republican National Convention, liberal columnist Molly Ivins opined, "probably sounded better in the original German." Her meaning was clear: She was identifying Buchanan as a "nazi," delegitimizing his nationalism and social conservatism with the most potent weapon in the Left's rhetorical arsenal.

So as racial nationalists we can either manufacture false "anti-racist" credentials by claiming to hate Hitler just as much as Abe Foxman does, a subterfuge that I very much doubt will convince anyone, least of all Abe, or we can tell the truth.

The truth is that the maniacal Hitler of popular demonology is a World War II propaganda fiction, and the principal purpose of the fiction's incessant repetition more than fifty years after the war is to stigmatize any nationalist movement, NS or otherwise. Hitler now represents not a specific historical figure and the political party he led, but nationalism of any variety, from timid anti-immigration conservatives to angry White-power skinheads. The System's anti-Hitler orthodoxy, invoked almost daily, is in effect tacit propaganda for multiracialism and a potent device to keep all nationalists perpetually hiding in closets, too afraid of labels like "racist" and "nazi" to openly say what we sincerely believe. We have, therefore, a real interest in demythologizing Hitler, and we have no hope of escaping our association with what he now represents. We can't run away from Hitler, however much some of us want to.

LET'S NOTICE THE OBVIOUS

The crucial facts about World War II are uncomplicated and readily available in mainstream sources. NS Germany had limited war aims: the recovery of territory taken from Germany at Versailles, the acquisition of living space for the German people in the East, and the destruction of the Marxist Soviet Union, history's most brutal regime. Insofar as the United States had any stake at all in the outcome of the war, it would have been to help Germany and her Axis allies, including thousands of Russian patriots, accomplish the latter. Absent the campaign conducted by the Western democracies to save Stalinism by defeating Hitler, the Soviet Union would have collapsed.

Since America had no national interests in the conflict in Europe, our government deliberately lied about German war aims in order to manufacture the perception that we did, claiming that Hitler had global territorial ambitions, a plan for "world domination." Over fifty years later, most Americans still accept the lies.

The predictable result of the Allied victory and the German defeat was Stalin's occupation of half of Europe. A war that ostensibly began to restore Polish sovereignty ended with Poland, along with the rest of Eastern Europe, being handed over to the Communists. And in quite concrete terms no American would have died in Vietnam if Hitler had destroyed Soviet Communism, arguably the central objective of his political career; American soldiers fought in Europe so that their sons could die in Southeast Asia.

None of this should be the least controversial. It is a symptom of the effect of persistent propaganda that so many of us fail to notice the obvious.

It is only a slight exaggeration to say that multiracialism itself, along with our servile deference to Jewry, is founded on the mythical image of Hitler as evil incarnate, Satan's secular counterpart in modern history. Remove the false, childishly simplistic Hitler myth, and a significant ideological justification for multiracialism would collapse. The simple question, "Were Hitler and NS Germany really as evil as everyone says?," therefore has huge repercussions, and an entire machinery of propaganda—ranging from Hollywood films and "Holocaust education" in the public schools to off-hand comments in the controlled media ("better in the original German")—has been designed to discourage anyone from even contemplating the obvious but heretical answer.

NATIONAL SOCIALISM

Hitler defined his own national socialism as a uniquely German movement: "The National Socialist doctrine, as I have always proclaimed, is not for export. It was conceived for the German people" (*Hitler-Bormann Documents*, February 21, 1945).

In other words, German National Socialism arose at a specific time in a specific place under the pressure of a unique set of historical circumstances, none of which could ever be precisely replicated elsewhere. In particular, the autocratic Führer state, central to NS Germany, would never be acceptable to Americans; our republican political culture and belief in individual rights are, thankfully, far too strong. Hitler was a dictator and his government authoritarian; Americans prefer their political and civil liberties.

Which doesn't mean that NS Germany was a police state. It had in fact fewer policemen *per capita*, and far fewer secret police, than either modern Germany or the United

States, despite the misleading image most of us have of legions of sinister Gestapo agents kicking down doors in the middle of the night.

The basic principles of national socialism are, nevertheless, universal: that God (or Nature) has assigned each of us to a racial group and has endowed each group with distinct qualities; that a nation is not simply a geographical concept, a set of lines arbitrarily drawn on a map irrespective of the people living within them, but instead derives (or should derive) its political institutions and national objectives from the character of the people themselves; that a nation organized to preserve a race and develop its distinctive character is therefore "natural"; that the strength and social cohesion of a nation derives from its sense of a common identity, of which race is the most important determinant; that in addition to our individual rights we have larger social obligations, not only to the present generation of our nation but to its past and future generations as well; that the primary purpose of a nation is not economic, but the preservation and advancement of its people, economics being subordinate to the *völkisch* (racial/national) objectives that should be a nation's core reason for existing.

"The [Nation-] State in itself," Hitler wrote, "has nothing whatsoever to do with any definite economic concept or a definite economic development. It does not arise from a compact made between contracting parties, within a certain delimited territory, for the purpose of serving economic ends. The State is a community of living beings who have kindred physical and spiritual natures, organized for the purpose of assuring the conservation of their own kind and to help towards fulfilling those ends which Providence has assigned to that particular race or racial branch" (*Mein Kampf*, I, iv).

In the generic sense of the term, national socialism is (arguably) not inconsistent with democratic institutions, despite Hitler's own view of the matter; its true antonyms are multiracialism and capitalist, one-world globalism. Nor is national socialism inconsistent with an American "melting pot" view of ethnicity, provided that the various ethnic groups that comprise the nation are sufficiently similar that each can see a common identity and common destiny in the others—that is, insofar as they, despite their ethnic differences, are branches of the same race and can, therefore, be effectively acculturated to a common set of national ideals.

I consider Hitler less a model to be followed than an avalanche of propaganda we must dig ourselves out from under. Never in human history has a single man received such sustained vilification, the basic effect and purpose of which has been to inhibit Whites from thinking racially and from acting in their own racial self-interest, as all other racial/ethnic groups do. Learning the truth about Hitler is a liberating experience. By the truth I mean not an idealized counter-myth to the pervasive myth of Hitler as evil incarnate, but the man himself, faults and virtues, strengths and weaknesses. Once you've done it, once you've discovered the real Hitler beneath the lies and distortions that have buried his legacy, you'll be permanently immunized against anti-White propaganda, because you will have seen through the best/worst the System has to offer.

http://library.flawlesslogic.com/hitler.htm

Racial Nationalism & the Aryans

Who Were the Aryans?

The Aryans were semi-nomadic Nordic Whites, perhaps located originally on the steppes of southern Russia and Central Asia, who spoke the parent language of the various Indo-European languages.

Latin, Greek, Hittite, Sanskrit, French, German, Latvian, English, Spanish, Russian, etc. are all Indo-European languages. Indo-European, or more properly Proto-Indo-European (PIE), is the lost ancestral language from which those languages ultimately derive. The "Proto" indicates that the grammar and vocabulary of this long extinct language, probably spoken up until 3000 BC, are a hypothetical reconstruction by modern philologists. Just as Romance languages like Italian and Spanish derive from Latin, so Latin derives from PIE.

Indo-European philology traditionally used "Aryan" both to denote a people, understood racially or ethnically, and the language group itself ("Aryan speech"), irrespective of the race or ethnicity of the people speaking its various branches. In the wake of National Socialist Germany's defeat, the term fell out of general scholarly use in both senses, and "Indo-European" (IE) became the preferred designation of the language group, "Indo-Europeans" of both the people who occupied the original Aryan homeland and their descendants, who gradually spread out across Europe, much of the Indian sub-continent, and parts of the Near East. Racial nationalists are not, of course, obliged to adopt the timid PC-lexicon of contemporary scholarship, but we should be aware of the imprecision of "Aryan" as a racial or ethnic classification.

Arya, meaning "noble," appears in various Indo-European languages. Its plural form (*Aryas* = "nobles") was probably the name the Aryans used to describe themselves prior to their dispersal, and it may survive in Eire (Ireland) and certainly survives in Iran (*Airyanam vaejo* = "realm of the Aryans"). The discovery of thousands of such cognate words in widely separated languages, along with similar grammatical structures, led philologists to conclude, early in the nineteenth century, that most European languages had evolved from a common proto-language spoken millennia ago by a distinct people who gradually left their original homeland in a series of migrations, carrying their language with them.

Traditionally Greek, Latin and Sanskrit were considered the closest languages to PIE, and much of the reconstructed Aryan proto-language is based on them. Modern Lithuanian, however, is the most archaic living language, closer to the original Aryan speech than any other. There is even an IE language, Tocharian, attested in Chinese Turkestan, which indicates that Aryans must have made an appearance in the Far East, a long-standing piece of linguistic evidence which has been recently confirmed by the discovery of the physical remains of a blond-haired people in China.

Perhaps the most famous proof for the prehistoric existence of PIE is the word for king: *rex* in Latin, *raja* in Sanskrit, *ri* in Old Irish, along with a host of other cognates. All are obviously variants of a common word for king. Since none of the peoples speaking these various languages were in physical contact with one another during the historical period—i.e. at a time for which written records exist—comparative philologists inferred that their respective languages must have evolved from a single proto-language, which is the only way of explaining the presence of the same word for "king" among such widely dispersed peoples. The Romans clearly didn't borrow *rex* from the Irish or the Indo-Aryans; each had instead inherited their own word for "king" from a common ancestral language.

Philologists can also, moreover, safely conclude that the Aryans must have had kings prior to emigrating from their original homeland in southern Russia. In fact a fairly detailed body of evidence about prehistoric Aryan political organization, marriage practices, and religious beliefs can be reconstructed on the basis of the survival of common vocabulary in the various extant Indo-European languages: They worshiped a sky-god, they traced descent through the male line, they raised cattle, they drank mead, they used horse-drawn chariots (which they probably invented) as weapons of war, etc. Even the red, white, and blue/green that appear in so many modern flags may have an Aryan pedigree. It is likely a survival from the Aryan tripartite social division of their communities into priests (white), warriors (red), and herders and cultivators (blue/green).

Aryans, or more specifically Indo-Aryans, make their first notable appearance in history around 2000–1500 BC as invaders of Northern India. The Sanskrit *Rig Veda*, a collection of religious texts still revered by modern Hindus, records (often enigmatically) their gradual subjugation of the dark-skinned inhabitants, the Dasyus: e.g. "Indra [= Norse Thor, Celtic Taranis] has torn open the fortresses of the Dasyus, which in their wombs hid the black people. He created land and water for Manu [= Aryan man]"; "lower than all besides, hast thou, O Indra, cast down the Dasyus, abject tribes of Dasas"; "after slaying the Dasyus, let Indra with his white friends win land, let him win the sun and water"; "Indra subdued the Dasyu color and drove it into hiding."

With all-outstripping chariot-wheel, O Indra,
Thou, far-famed, hast overthrown the twice ten kings

...
Thou goest from fight to fight, intrepidly
Destroying castle after castle here with strength.
—Rig Veda, 1.53

The Aryans were remarkably expansionist, and almost everywhere they went they conquered and subjugated the indigenous peoples, imposing their languages and (to varying degrees) their religious beliefs on the natives, and receiving in turn contributions from the peoples whom they conquered. Aryan invasions—or more accurately, a long sequence of different invasions by speakers of Indo-European languages—swept across Old Europe beginning as early as the fourth millennium BC, and over time the conquerors and the conquered melded into specific peoples with distinctive languages. Most of the contemporary inhabitants of Europe, along with their respective early national cultures, are the result of interaction between successive waves of Aryan invaders and culture of the particular White people that they conquered and with whom they later intermarried, and as a result almost all modern European languages are members of the Western branch of the IE family tree.

The birth of a European culture, however, predates the arrival of the Indo-Europeans. The cave art of Lascaux, which some have identified as the first flowering of Western man's creative genius, was the work of Old Europeans, as were Stonehenge in the North and the Minoan Palace culture of Crete in the South. A pan-European religious symbolism had already evolved, much of which was later incorporated into IE mythologies, including various regional adaptations of the ubiquitous Old European reverence for the Mother Goddess. Many of the principal figures in Greek mythology predate the arrival of Aryans, and during the course of ancient history Old European religious beliefs and practices continually reasserted themselves.

Europe is European because the conquerors and the conquered were members the same White race, different branches on the same family tree; India is a morass of poverty because the bulk of the conquered, with whom the Indo-Aryans eventually intermarried, were non-White Veddoids. The lesson is obvious. Even today high-caste Hindus can still be identified by their Caucasian features and light skin, and the poorest and most backward parts of India are generally the darkest.

As an aside, recent genetic studies have indicated that the Basques of Aquitaine and the Pyrenees are probably the purest form of Old Europeans as they existed prior to the arrival of Indo-European invaders. They evidently emerged from the invasions of Europe unconquered, and they remained sufficiently isolated to retain their own unique, non-IE language.

WHAT SHOULD WE CALL OURSELVES?

The history of the Aryans, of which the preceding is a necessarily simplifying summary, is not merely an interesting curiosity; it has important implications for how we define ourselves. A German, for example, is Aryan only insofar as the original inhabitants of ancient Germany were conquered by invaders who spoke an Indo-European language. In no significantly genetic sense can he be called a pure Aryan. Even at the time of the Indo-European invasions of Old Europe the term had lost much of its original meaning as the name of a distinct ethnic group. During their successive migrations from their homeland the Aryans had absorbed other White populations and had acquired often distinctive physiognomies, along with mutually incomprehensible (though related) languages.

Racialist writing is often contaminated by a divisive

Nordicism and a quasi-mystical adoration of the Aryan, and Hitler himself often used "Aryan" and "Nordic" interchangeably. But contrary to popular belief National Socialist race theorists never claimed that Germans were Aryans nor even that the bulk of the Germanic gene pool was Aryan. They argued, rather, that Nordics were more genetically Aryan than, say, Mediterranean Italians—a much more modest claim which has the additional virtue of being true. Northern Europe was sparsely populated prior to the Indo-European migrations into it, whereas Southern Europe already had an existing civilization and a much larger population. A Nordic German or Swede can thus rightly say that he is more Aryan than a Greek or a southern Italian, but he shouldn't bother doing it, since the distinction is by now so immaterial that it only serves to divide Whites.

For the term Aryan to have any validity in a contemporary context, it can only denote members of the European cultures that arose from the interaction of IE-speaking ("Aryan") invaders and the White Europeans who preceded them. It cannot mean Aryans proper, since no such people, in the strict sense, have existed for at least two thousand years.

An additional difficulty with "Aryan," even if it is used in this loose sense, is that it still excludes a fair number of people most of us would consider White. In addition to Basque, Finnish and Hungarian are also not Indo-European languages, and neither Finns nor Hungarians are descendants of a people who spoke PIE. Yet both are obviously White.

"White" is thus preferable to "Aryan" as a name for the race whose existence we must secure, but White is also imperfect. We should never fetishize minor racial differences by turning insignificant gradations in "whiteness" into a hierarchy of relative degrees of racial purity. Most Italians, Greeks, and Spaniards are members of the Mediterranean branch of our White race, and they are generally somewhat darker than Nordics. Most Ashkenazi Jews are, conversely, physically more "white" than the average Greek. Yet these "white" Jews are the principal subverters of Western civilization, whereas Greeks, Italians, and Spaniards are among its principal creators.

What we really need is some classificatory term that indicates "non-Jewish people of European descent." Unfortunately no such term exists. "White" and "Aryan" are acceptable substitutes only if we understand their deficiencies.

Euro-American racial nationalism differs markedly from the more ethnically based nationalisms of Europe. In Europe ethnic distinctions among Whites are a valuable political tool for preserving a "Europe of nations" against the forces of capitalist globalization and Third World immigration. But on this continent we are—for good or ill, and I think for good—an amalgam of different European ethnicities, despite our undoubted Anglo-Celtic cultural and legal core. It is inevitable, though unfortunate, that under these circumstances racialists will sometimes quibble among ourselves about the exact contours of the category "White," that is, which ethnic groups are part of *us* and which are not. Yet what cannot be disputed, at least by anyone who wants to be constructive about the racialist movement on this continent, is that we all must define ourselves as Euro-American or perish. Otherwise we are simply an unconnected series of disparate ethnic groups, defenseless against a consciously anti-White "rainbow coalition" that aims to bury us all.

http://library.flawlesslogic.com/concept.htm

Holocaust Commemoration

Lessons in Tolerance

Steven Spielberg's *Schindler's List* concludes with a sentimental epigraph, labeled as a quotation from the Talmud: "Whoever saves one life, saves the world entire." This declaration of humane universalism is appealing to many, and it became part of the publicity campaign for the film, but it is not genuinely Jewish. As historian Peter Novick reports, in his informative *The Holocaust in American Life*, "the traditional version, the one taught in all Orthodox yeshivot, speaks of 'whoever saves one life of Israel.'" The traditional Talmudic text thus stands in stark contrast to Spielberg's epigraph. To save one Jewish life ("one life of Israel") is to save the entire world, because in Jehovah's eyes Jewish lives are infinitely precious and non-Jewish lives are not. Far from teaching the brotherhood of man, the Talmud teaches a Jewish supremacy so absolute that a single Jewish life is deemed as valuable as the totality of all other lives.[1]

---

[1] Peter Novick, *The Holocaust in American Life* (Boston: Houghton Mifflin, 1999), 182–83. The Talmudic aphorism is from the Mishnah, Sanhedrin 4.5. In a standard scholarly translation—*The Mishnah*, trans. Herbert Danby (Oxford: Oxford University Press 1933)—it reads: "If any man has caused a single soul to perish from Israel Scripture imputes it to him as though he had caused a whole world to perish; and if any man saves alive a single soul from Israel Scripture imputes it to him as though he had saved alive a whole world." On the subject of Jewish ethnocentrism, the comments of the Talmudic scholar Rabbi Yitzhak Ginsburgh, a former American citizen now living in Israel, are worth noting: "If every single cell in a Jewish

The Talmud, Judaism's most sacred document, exists in two major recensions. The apparently universalist text that *Schindler's List* quotes appears in the Jerusalem Talmud, the strikingly ethnocentric text in the authoritative Babylonian Talmud. The latter, the real Talmud, contains the definitive text taught in all Orthodox religious schools and memorized by generations of studious young Jews, but less than a moment's reflection will disclose the practical impossibility of including, in a film addressed to a non-Jewish audience, a Talmudic aphorism that so markedly depreciates non-Jewish lives. Spielberg prudently chose instead to present Judaism as a universalist faith with an extravagant notion of the value of each individual life, a Semitic brand of Christianity. He was not teaching a Jewish moral lesson but rather an exaggerated piece of Christian humanism, Talmudic tribal wisdom turned on its head for the educational benefit of non-Jews, reflecting their religious traditions, not his own.[2]

---

body entails divinity, and is thus part of God, then every strand of DNA is a part of God. Therefore, something is special about Jewish DNA. . . . If a Jew needs a liver, can he take the liver of an innocent non-Jew to save him? The Torah would probably permit that. Jewish life has an infinite value. There is something more holy and unique about Jewish life than about non-Jewish life." Quoted in Israel Shahak and Norton Mezvinsky, *Jewish Fundamentalism in Israel* (London: Pluto Press, 1999), 43.

[2] For a religious Jew the two different versions of the Talmudic aphorism that Spielberg quotes would be identical in meaning, since the scriptural exegesis of classical Judaism regularly interprets superficially universal moral principles in exclusivist terms, with apparently generic language like "neighbor" and "thy fellow (man)" referring only to Jews. Traditional Jewish moral teachings assign great value to saving Jewish lives, but actually prohibit Jews from saving the lives of Gentiles, except in circumstances where inaction might pro-

The chasm between genuine Talmudic ethnocentrism and Spielberg's bogus Talmudic universalism reveals some significant issues in the marketing of the Jewish Holocaust. In the Diaspora, where Jews form small minorities among their host populations, public commemoration of Jewish deaths during World War II cannot explicitly privilege Jewish lives over other lives, however much Jewish propagandists wish that it could. It must instead teach universalist lessons filled with attractive humanitarian ideals, lessons that offer the promise of moral improvement to anyone who successfully internalizes them. We become better by watching *Schindler's List*, learning the infinite value of all human life and the moral obligation to respect minority differences, just as we become better by visiting Holocaust museums, where the same lessons are taught.

Yet moral improvement effected by commemorating

---

voke hostility. See Israel Shahak, *Jewish History, Jewish Religion: The Weight of Three Thousand Years* (London: Pluto Press, 1994), 36–37, 80–81. The Babylonian Talmud is, in any case, the authoritative recension of the rabbinical writings that constitute Judaism's central religious text. See Solomon Grayzel, *A History of the Jews* (Philadelphia: Jewish Publication Society of America, 1947), 214–15, 231ff. For Christian universalism versus Jewish particularism, see Acts 10.1–35 ("a Jew is contaminated if he consorts with one of another race, or visits him"; Knox) and Acts 15.7–11. For Old Testament fantasies of conquest and domination, see Exodus 17.14–16 and 1 Samuel 15.2–3 (Amalek, Israel's generic Gentile enemy); Deuteronomy 12.2–3 and 20.15–18 (Israel's fanaticism); and Isaiah 49.22–23 ("they shall bow down to you and lick the dust of your feet"; RSV). For Jewish blood purity, see Deuteronomy 7.1–6 and Joshua 23.12–13. For the Jewish poetry of racial revenge, see the remarkable Psalm 137 ("happy shall he be who takes your little ones [i.e infants] and dashes them against the rock!"; RSV).

Jewish deaths is only a more subtle form of the same tribal ethnocentrism that Spielberg sought to conceal. In contemporary America and throughout much of the West an acknowledged legacy of victimization in the past is a source of political power in the present, and incessant commemoration of the Jewish Holocaust is, as Novick puts it, the reward for winning a "gold medal in the Victimization Olympics," an official recognition of preeminent victimhood that makes Jews more politically powerful even while we and they jointly remember their wartime powerlessness. Commemorating Jewish weakness sixty years ago is tantamount to celebrating Jewish strength today. Holocaust commemoration tells us, moreover, that Jewish deaths in World War II were much more significant than other deaths, since collectively they constitute a unique archive of invaluable universal truths, although during their lives most of the Holocaust's non-survivors were themselves perfectly indifferent to the universal truths that their deaths would later be made to teach.

The public discourse of the Holocaust can therefore only be tortuously deceptive, since its underlying motive is, as Norman Finkelstein argues, "Jewish aggrandizement," while its overt message is human brotherhood, a universal truth that Judaism, history's most radically ethnocentric religion, has wisely never acknowledged.[3]

"American Jews," says Rabbi Michael Berenbaum, a former director of the US Holocaust Memorial Museum (USHMM), "reinforce their commitment to pluralism by recalling the atrocities that sprang from intolerance."[4] The

---

[3] Norman Finkelstein, *The Holocaust Industry: Reflections on the Exploitation of Jewish Suffering* (New York: Verso, 2000), 8.

[4] Quoted in Edward Norden, "Yes and No to the Holocaust Museums," *Commentary* 96, no. 2 (August 1993), 32.

claim that institutionalized recollection of German intolerance and German atrocities will foster American pluralism takes us beyond pious sentiments about human brotherhood. Speaking in code, a code not yet deciphered by most Whites, Berenbaum was cautiously stating American Jewry's longstanding commitment to racial balkanization ("pluralism") through multiculturalism and non-White immigration, both of which, because they dissolve Euro-America's race-cultural cohesiveness, are in the perceived group interests of American Jewry.

The Jewish Holocaust serves as multiracialism's reigning mythology. Since racial balkanization plainly does not benefit the Euro-American majority, our evolving multiracial anti-nation requires some overarching myth that inhibits the expression of majority group interests. A political regime whose survival depends on White passivity must discredit White self-assertion, and the Holocaust helps achieve that objective by teaching Whites to fear their own interests while deferring to the interests of others. The Jewish aggrandizement implicit in Holocaust commemoration must, however, remain concealed beneath the opaque language of tolerance. Systematic deception is the price Jews pay to maintain the improbable fiction of their selfless commitment to pluralism.

The glaring flaw in the Holocaust's discourse of tolerance, the point at which Jewish self-interest becomes most apparent, is Israel, the world's only openly racialist nation, an ethnostate dedicated not to tolerance and pluralism and scrupulous avoidance of atrocities, but to the preservation and advancement of a single *Volk*, the Jewish people. Israel won its very existence through a violent assertion of racial will inconsistent with the racial passivity that Holocaust lessons mandate. Most Israeli towns once had Arab names, as Moshe Dayan candidly acknowledged. At now *Arab-rein* Samariah, a former Palestinian town whose indigenous population was expelled during Israel's War of Independence, Jews have brazenly erected a Holocaust museum dedicated to anti-nazi ghetto fighters, a commemoration of old Jewish weakness that sanctifies the effects of new Jewish strength. "The heart of every *authentic* response to the Holocaust," writes philosopher Emil Fackenheim, ". . . is a commitment to the autonomy and security of the State of Israel."[5] *Schindler's List* accordingly ends in Jewry's Mideast refuge from European hatred, indicating that all the preceding trials and travails of the film's Jewish survivors teach a specifically Zionist lesson.

In the West the lessons of the Jewish Holocaust prescribe multiculturalism and Third World immigration; for Israel, the Jewish state, they prescribe the exact opposite, teaching the right of Jews to live among other Jews within their own autonomous nation, protected from contaminating pluralism by a Jews-only immigration policy. "The world," Alan Dershowitz believes, "owes Jews, and the Jewish state, which was built on the ashes of the Holocaust, a special understanding."[6] Jewish nationalism is

---

[5] For Dayan, see Edward Said, *The Question of Palestine* (New York: Vintage, 1979), 14; for the Ghetto Fighters Museum at Samariah, see Tom Segev, *The Seventh Million: The Israelis and the Holocaust*, trans. Haim Watzman (New York: Hill & Wang, 1993), 450–51; Emil Fackenheim, "The Holocaust and the State of Israel: Their Relation," in *EJ Yearbook* (Jerusalem: Keter, 1974), 154f, quoted in Leni Yahil, *The Holocaust: The Fate of European Jewry* (Oxford: Oxford University Press, 1990), 6. Since 1973 America's masochistic "commitment to the autonomy and security of the State of Israel" has cost taxpayers about $1.6 trillion, according to the estimate of economist Thomas Stauffer. See David R. Francis, "Economist Tallies Swelling Cost of Israel to US," *Christian Science Monitor*, December 9, 2002.

[6] Alan Dershowitz, *Chutzpah* (Boston: Little, Brown, 1991), 136.

sanctioned by the Holocaust and merits our special understanding; other nationalisms, especially White nationalisms, are morally prohibited.

Blu Greenberg, wife of Rabbi Irving Greenberg, an influential advocate of American Holocaust commemoration, once believed that Jewish wartime suffering should remain an internal group memory, sacred to Jews alone, but quickly changed her opinion after attending an interfaith Holocaust service, where she found it "moving and comforting to see Christians share tears with us, acknowledge Christian guilt, and commit themselves to the security of Israel."[7] Christian tears and Christian guilt equal Jewish power, as Blu Greenberg recognized, yet tears of guilt yield more valuable political benefits than do mere tears of commiseration. Our willingness to accept guilt and American Jewry's eagerness to assign it jointly form the precondition of all the Holocaust's meanings and the glue that holds them together in a largely uncontested set of often contradictory lessons.

The public discourse of the Jewish Holocaust is incoherent: it speaks in the universalist language of tolerance and inclusion, while justifying Jewish particularism in Israel; it claims to find in stories of Jewish wartime suffering distinctively Jewish humanitarian lessons, applicable to everyone everywhere, while borrowing them from the historical religion of the West; it teaches human brotherhood, while elevating the suffering of Jews far above all other suffering; it commemorates Jewish powerlessness, while demonstrating Jewish power. But beneath all its deceptions and contradictions lies the message of broad Western responsibility for German mistreatment of Jews,

---

[7] Blu Greenberg, "Talking to Kids about the Holocaust," in Roselyn Bell, *The Hadassah Magazine Jewish Parenting Book* (New York, 1989), 247, quoted in Novick, 208.

a special culpability which Rabbi Eliezer Berkovits, a self-styled Holocaust theologian, has called "the measureless Christian guilt toward the Jewish people."[8]

Institutionalized Holocaust commemoration in the United States presupposes that White Americans are notably deficient in the various moral qualities that Holocaust remembering purportedly inculcates, whereas Jews, owing to their group experience of nazi persecution, are the appropriate teachers of necessary lessons in racial tolerance. Those peculiar meanings did not, needless to say, arise unaided from stories of German atrocities against European Jewry. The truth of our collective guilt required an aggressive reinterpretation of the Second World War, an assault on the moral legitimacy of the Western nations that fought and won it. Through a remarkable transformation, the Allied victors have become co-agents in the crimes and alleged crimes of the regime they defeated, and the war itself has been reimagined as a Judeocentric moral test, which all of us conspicuously failed. Our measureless guilt, together with the entire edifice of Holocaust commemoration erected upon it, is a doctrine of moral equivalence projected back into the past in order to shape the present.

AN EARLY HOLOCAUST LESSON

In 1944, as the war in Europe was drawing to a close,

---

[8] Eliezer Berkovits, "Rewriting the History of the Holocaust," *Sh'ma* 10, no. 198 (1980), available from http://www.clal.org/e57.html. Cf. Berkovits, *Faith After the Holocaust* (New York: Ktav, 1973), 127: "Israel was God's question of destiny to Christendom. In its answer, the Christian world failed him tragically. Through Israel God tested Western man and found him wanting. This gruesome failure of Christianity has led the Western world to the greatest moral debacle of any civilization—the holocaust."

Jewish playwright Arthur Miller, then in his late twenties, sat down to write *Focus*, his first and only novel. It would be a critical moral fable about his fellow Americans, for Miller did not share the heroic self-image and traditional patriotism that characterized most other Americans during the war years. *Focus*, published in 1945, would be an imaginative elaboration of a very simple thesis: being a Jew in Roosevelt's America was like being a Jew in Hitler's Germany. In their irrational hatred of the Jewish Other, White Americans, the same White Americans who were then fighting fascism in Europe and the Far East, were no different from nazis.

Lawrence Newman, the novel's WASP protagonist, is a corporate personnel manager whose quiet bourgeois world is permanently disrupted after he begins to wear eyeglasses, which strangely make him look Jewish, a dangerous liability in the America of Miller's fertile imagination. Without glasses Newman is a gray-flannelled Episcopalian, a normal White American, despite his ethnically ambiguous surname; with glasses he is perceived and treated as a despised Jew, persecuted and even attacked by other normal White Americans, all of whom are racist and anti-Semitic, as Newman had been before he gained his factitious Jewishness.

The novel's organizing narrative conceit, that eyeglasses can turn an anti-Semitic Gentile into a Jew, conveys an obvious Judeocentric meaning: Lawrence Newman, in his culpable blindness to the intolerance that surrounds him, must first be *seen* as a Jew in order to *see* clearly. Thus in his new role as a reluctant Jew, now seeing and experiencing the world through the Jewish lenses conferred by his racial marginalization, Newman gradually discovers that his largely homogeneous New York neighborhood, which had once seemed a benign social milieu, is in reality, despite its placid surface, a seething cauldron of xenophobia and hate, at least for anyone with the misfortune to be different, or in his case merely to appear different. "Behind these snug, flat-roofed houses," Newman now perceives, "a sharp-tipped and murderous monster was nightly being formed, and its eyes were upon him."[9]

The novel's historical context is central to its subject. In *Focus* the European war, depicted in our propaganda as a titanic struggle of good against evil, seems little more than a distant contest between two rival groups of pogromists, each nurturing its own "murderous monster" of racial hatred. In Europe German nazis conduct mass hangings of Jews, while at home angry anti-Semites, organized into the Christian Front, part of a large network of patriotic organizations spread across the country, beat Jews and rape Puerto Ricans as they await the return of the American military, who will then assume the lethal role of storm troops in driving Jews from America, beginning first in New York, the center of Jew-hatred. White America's cleansing war against Jewry will begin, as an activist neighbor informs Newman, "when the boys come home," since American combatants in the European war are at one with their German enemies in their implacable anti-Semitism.

In the political environment we now all inhabit, nothing in *Focus* is startling, nothing would be out of place in a sensitivity workshop or an anti-racialist educational exercise. The novel's vision of a virulently racist America would have appeared radical in 1945; now it is commonplace, especially for young Whites immersed in a rigorous program of multicultural miseducation. Miller, alarmed by the failure of non-Jews to comprehend "the threatening existence of Nazism," and unimpressed by the fact that many men of his age cohort were then dying in Eu-

---

[9] Arthur Miller, *Focus* (1945; New York: Penguin, 2001), 178.

rope fighting Germans, took it upon himself to teach an early version of what would eventually become the most insidious of the Jewish Holocaust's numerous lessons, namely that pathological ("nazi") hatreds lurk behind the West's superficially civilized exterior.

Whereas American wartime propaganda had, naturally enough, presented NS Germany as the moral antonym of the United States in particular and of the democratic West in general, Miller substituted a much different contrastive structure, placing innocent Jews on one side and lethally malevolent Whites on the other, with racial minorities like Blacks and Puerto Ricans in ancillary roles as occasional victims of White intolerance. This structure, which Miller may have been the first to discover, conflated Germans and their enemies in order to nazify White Gentiles as a whole. *Focus* was a thorough defamation of Euro-America for its endemic anti-Semitism and racial hatred, the purpose of which was to efface any significant moral distinction between ourselves and the propaganda image of the Nazi. Miller's nazification required the Nazi as the acknowledged representation of evil, but his concrete targets were White Americans, who had not yet seen their own visible racial pathologies.

Gratitude has never been a Jewish character trait. "The threatening existence of Nazism," anyone unfamiliar with Jewish idiosyncrasies might think, should have encouraged Arthur Miller to reflect upon the very significant differences that distinguished Hitler's Germany from Roosevelt's America, and to count his blessings. NS Germany, committed to the elimination of Jewish influence from German society, was a systematically anti-Semitic regime; the United States was not. American anti-Semitism, despite Miller's wildly paranoid fears, had never become a serious political force, and any reasonable litany of Jewish complaints against Euro-Americans would have been brief: country clubs that excluded Jews; one prominent lynching, of convicted child-killer Leo Frank; a general irritation at Jewish vulgarity; a well-justified suspicion of Jewish business practices; occasional complaints about the Jewish affection for Marxism and political subversion, also well-justified.[10] No pogroms, no organized violence, none of the systematic anti-Semitism that Jewish group behavior has often produced.

The remarkable ease with which organized Jewry successfully pilloried Charles Lindbergh, over his mild criticism of Jewish agitation for American entry into the European Civil War, is a telling case in point: in a contest between the power of the label "anti-Semite" and the prestige of America's most admired national hero, the national hero came out the loser. The United States was, as Adolf Hitler observed, the Jews' "new hunting grounds," a tolerant environment surprisingly conducive to Jewish interests; but Miller refused to acknowledge his good fortune, since that would have required a tacit compliment for the White American nation he so passionately hated.

Focus, with its often cartoonish didacticism, is no literary landmark. It was, however, a profoundly prophetic novel, and it helpfully illustrates how the ideological destination of the Jewish Holocaust, the Judeocentric anti-racialism that Holocaust commemoration would later teach, was already implicit in the ethnic discontents and

---

[10] Cf. David Horowitz, *Radical Son: A Generational Odyssey* (New York: The Free Press, 1997), 44: "It was not my parents' idealism that elicited fear and provoked hostility from the *goyim*. It was their hostility toward the *goyim*, and indeed everything the *goyim* held dear, that incited the hostility back." Horowitz, now a neo-conservative activist with a passionate commitment to Israel, was an important New Left ideologue in the 1960s; his parents were Stalinists.

cultural estrangement of American Jewry. An imaginative Jew writing before the liberation of the German concentration camps could arrive at nazifying Holocaust propaganda without the Holocaust, which suggests that the Holocaust does not represent events during the Second World War but rather reveals Jewish attitudes toward their benefactors. The Holocaust, as an idea, was latent Jewish racial aggression awaiting both a symbol and an opportunity to express itself.

THE NAZI CAMPS

In April of 1945 Dwight Eisenhower, Supreme Allied Commander in Western Europe, ordered troops under his command to tour Ohrdruf, a sub-camp of Buchenwald and the first concentration camp on German soil to be liberated. He had an educational purpose in mind: "We are told that the American soldier does not know what he is fighting for. Now, at least, he will know what he is fighting *against*."

General Eisenhower was not alone in believing that the camps lent moral clarity to the war in Europe. Anti-nazi propaganda had ascribed to Germans a host of malevolent qualities distinguishing *them* from *us*: arrogance, cruelty, blind obedience to criminal orders, unprovoked violence against the defenseless. Like most modern war propaganda, it had externalized evil in the enemy, thereby bestowing heroic goodness on all the enemy's enemies, the Western democracies and their gallant Soviet ally. The liberated camps, with their legions of emaciated corpses and often skeletal inmates, were vivid confirmation of German darkness and Allied light. The nazi concentration camp retroactively provided, as Novick remarks, "the symbol that defined the meaning of the war."[11] American

---

[11] Novick, 85. The liberators, of course, misunderstood their

soldiers could now see with their own eyes solid evidence of the evil they had been fighting against.

Sixty years after the event we now generally assume that American and British liberators of German concentration camps were witnesses to the "Holocaust" and that the inmates whom they liberated were its Jewish "survivors." That assumption, as Novick points out, is a mistake, our own retrospective interpretation of the evidence, a misinterpretation shaped by the centrality that the Holocaust, a term none of the liberators would have understood, has acquired in our collective consciousness. In photographs of camp survivors we now *see* Jews, but in the spring of 1945 Allied soldiers did not see Jews in the flesh-and-blood inmates they liberated. They saw political prisoners and resistance fighters, "the men of all nations that Hitler's agents had picked out as prime opponents of Nazism," as a reporter for *Life* described the inmates in Dachau.

Most journalistic accounts of the liberation of the camps spoke in similar language; "Jew" did not appear anywhere in Edward R. Murrow's famous radio broadcast from Buchenwald. "There was nothing," Novick writes, "about the reporting on the liberation of the camps that treated Jews as more than *among* the victims of the Nazis; nothing that suggested the camps were emblematic

---

discovery. Cf. Mark Weber, "Buchenwald: Legend and Reality," *JHR* [= *Journal of Historical Review*] 7, no. 4 (Winter 1986), 411: "The great majority of those who died at Buchenwald perished during the chaotic final months of the war. They succumbed to disease, often aggravated by malnutrition, in spite of woefully inadequate efforts to keep them alive. They were victims, not of an 'extermination' program, but rather of the terrible overcrowding and severe lack of food and medical supplies due to a general collapse of order in Germany during the tumultuous final phase of the war."

of anything other than Nazi barbarism in general; nothing, that is, that associated them with what is now designated 'the Holocaust.'"[12] The horror camps, as Eisenhower called them, were not evidence of nazi "racism" nor were their inmates "survivors" of a genocidal Final Solution against Jews. The camps were instead the results of nazi dictatorship, evidence of political crimes against anti-nazis that served by contrast to confirm Anglo-American traditions of political liberty. Godless German fascists were visibly capable of such crimes against political opponents, whereas we, in the democratic West, were not.

In one important respect their interpretation then was much closer to the truth than ours now: only about a fifth of the prisoners liberated by Americans were Jews. The majority by far were non-Jews, some of them real resistance fighters, many apolitical criminals, many others Communists interned for the duration of the war as political enemies of the anti-Marxist NS Reich. Although our eyes have been trained to see, in photographs and old newsreels of Dachau and Buchenwald, Jews targeted for racial destruction, our eyes deceive. Jews formed the majority of internees in German concentration camps in the East, notably at Auschwitz, but not in the camps on German soil and thus not in the camps that Americans liberated. For Americans in 1945, the human face of the nazi concentration camp was expressed, for the most part, in photographs of European Gentiles, not dead Jews. The prevailing political view of the camps, which saw their inmates as brave co-belligerents in our crusade against nazi tyranny, was perfectly convincing.[13]

It should be superfluous to mention that none of the

---

[12] Novick, 65.

[13] On the ethnic composition of the camp inmates, see Appendix 1 below.

American liberators felt culpable, none felt that they were somehow complicit in the carnage before them, none felt that they should shed tears of contrition for the victims. Some humanitarians warned of publicizing photographic evidence of nazi atrocities for fear that it might inflame a spirit of vengeance against prostrate Germany; no one worried that nazi atrocities would induce feelings of guilt among the victors for having failed to prevent them or for having been part of the cultural system that perpetrated them. *Our* side, the democratic West, had just defeated *them*, the fascist dictatorships. Dachau and Buchenwald testified to *our* goodness and *their* evil. Liberty had defeated tyranny. It was a polarizing and triumphalist interpretation, befitting the victors of history's most destructive conflict.

Our world would be a better place today if Germany and her allies had won the war in Europe; it would be an immensely better place if the war had never been fought in the first place. Yet given the war's unrecoverable finality in 1945, the triumphalist victors' narrative was a reasonable interpretation of an unnecessary bloodletting, at least if you belonged to any of the nations that had fought on the winning side of Europe's Civil War. If you were a German, our perception of your evil was a terrible libel against you and your descendants. A war's losers, however, seldom write the history of their defeat. History is usually written by the victors, and our victors' history served our parochial interests. It said something good about ourselves, and it dignified the many Allied lives that the fratricidal European war had needlessly cost.

BROADENING GUILT

Eisenhower, after his visit to Ohrdruf, wrote a letter to General George Marshall: "The things I saw beggar description. . . . The visual evidence and the verbal testimony of starvation, cruelty and bestiality were so overpowering. . . . I made the visit deliberately, in order to be in a position to give first hand evidence of these things if ever, in the future, there develops a tendency to charge these allegations merely to propaganda."

Eisenhower's words are chiseled into the stone of the USHMM's exterior wall, providing Gentile validation of the Judeocentrism enshrined within. The words are true — that is, General Eisenhower actually wrote them — but they have now been appropriated into a much different discourse, Jewish Holocaust discourse, so that in their new context, as part of a monument on American soil commemorating Jewish wartime suffering in Europe, Eisenhower is made to speak of the Holocaust, the industrially planned extermination of six million Jews, a racial rather than a political crime. The difference is substantial, not simply a new label attached to old events. For the Jewish Holocaust is the attenuation and even the displacement of the heroic version of the Second World War — the version that, rightly or not, the Allied soldiers who fought and died winning it believed — in favor of another version, a Jewish version that imputes to the victors the same sins as the vanquished. Whereas the men who liberated the camps thought that they had, like St. George killing the dragon, brought an end to an evil, in the Holocaust discourse that would emerge twenty years later they had merely uncovered their own moral failure, whose source still must be eradicated.

European Jews were killed not only by Germans but also by "apathy" and "silence" in the United States and Great Britain, the apathy and silence being products of a pervasive anti-Semitism that the Anglo-American world shared with its German enemies. This staple of Holocaust discourse, repeated in many forms by many Jewish authors, is a transparently *ad hoc* attempt to surmount a large, inconvenient obstacle: the Western Allies did not themselves kill European Jews. The allegation that Hitler attempted genocide, the physical extermination of all Jews, might have remained politically inert, useful for extracting reparations from Germany but providing no special advantages in the United States, unless it could be framed so inclusively that our racial intolerance, an ocean away from Auschwitz, could be numbered among its causes. Thus in addition to polemical studies situating the Holocaust as the culmination of a long history of European anti-Semitism, there has emerged in recent decades a growing body of equally polemical scholarship, with titles like *The Jews Were Expendable* and *The Abandonment of the Jews*, inculpating the Allies, and in particular the United States, for their failure to prevent the Holocaust. With the outbreak of the European war, the fate of six million Jews fell into the hands of the American government, and the American government, reflecting the anti-alien bigotry of the American people, deliberately allowed them to die.[14]

---

[14] Paraphrasing here the PBS documentary *America and the Holocaust: Deceit and Indifference* (WGBH Educational Foundation, 1994): "In the spring of 1940, the fate of European Jews now fell into the hands of a new Roosevelt appointee, Assistant Secretary of State Breckinridge Long. . . . Long endorsed the anti-alien bigotry of the times." *America and the Holocaust*, based on influential Holocaust scholarship, was written and produced by Martin Ostrow and boasted a wealth of well-known Jewish scholars (including Deborah Lipstadt) on its academic panel. The deliberate "abandonment of the Jews" also figures prominently in Herman Wouk's 1978 novel *War and Remembrance*, which gave fictional expression to the charge that American anti-Semitism caused the Holocaust. The most popular Jewish inculpation of the British invokes their reluctance to permit European Jews to displace Arabs in Palestine, their motive being (unsurprisingly) anti-Semitism.

In their failure to rescue Jews, USHMM spokesman Helen Fagin charged a decade ago, Americans were "just as guilty" as Jew-killing Germans.[15] Fagin was summarizing, more bluntly than most official Holocaust propagandists, an ideological revolution that had transformed the German concentration camp from specific evidence of nazi tyranny into a symbol of generalized White guilt. She was also stating the implicit justification for her museum. White schoolchildren visit the USHMM, along with dozens of similar institutions, not to honor American wartime heroism or to recapture the moral certainty that the camps once evoked, but to learn the lessons of their ancestral culpability, discovering how our old selective ("racist") immigration laws and our willful failure to save Jews caused the Holocaust, both claims being important elements in the museum's educational mission. Many of the same photographs that Americans saw in 1945 are reproduced, and the physical form of the camps therefore remains similar, but their moral content has been dramatically altered. *We* have become complicit in the events that "Holocaust" designates.

"If you are brought up a Jew," the anthropologist Ashley Montagu (Israel Ehrenberg) once opined, "you know that all non-Jews are anti-Semitic."[16] Accordingly at the Simon Wiesenthal Center's Museum of Tolerance in Los Angeles, which teaches "the dynamics of racism and prejudice in America and the history of the Holocaust,"

---

[15] *ABC World News Tonight*, April 21, 1993, quoted in Novick, 48. Prof. Fagin, a Holocaust pedagogue who specializes in European anti-Semitism and Holocaust literature, was the chair of the USHMM's Education Committee.

[16] Quoted in Kevin MacDonald, *The Culture of Critique: An Evolutionary Analysis of Jewish Involvement in Twentieth-Century Intellectual and Political Movements* (Westport, Conn.: Praeger, 1998), 26.

visitors must enter the various educational exhibits by passing through a door marked "Prejudiced" in red neon lights. Although another door is marked "Not Prejudiced," for those who imagine they should be allowed to tour the museum without accepting racial guilt, that second door cannot in fact be opened. It is locked, a fraudulent object lesson encapsulating the Holocaust's core antiracialist meaning. Our moral deficiencies—our "racism" and our "prejudices"—are central to the Holocaust's subject matter, and we cannot learn tolerance, and cannot even tour the Tolerance Museum, without first acknowledging them. Since prejudice against others is often roughly equivalent to a preference for one's own, Holocaust education nazifies the politically dangerous White racial cohesion it threatens. "Prejudice," we must learn, is an especially wicked condition, and all of us, our Jewish instructors excepted, are afflicted with it.

In the Tolerance Museum, run by militantly Zionist Orthodox Jews, Columbus and the Pilgrim Fathers keep company, as examples of genocidal intolerance, with Hitler, Saddam Hussein and Pol Pot, which is a good indication of the scale of the museum's political ambitions. Not only our present deficiencies but even our pre-national origins must be reinterpreted in the Holocaust's massive shadow, our old offenses against the canons of tolerance serving as harbingers of the infinitely greater crime to follow. Within this Holocaust-centered historiography the lives and the prejudices of our ancestors become prefigurations of nazi crimes against Jews, a model of history that can accommodate the commemoration of any number of crimes against various racial minorities, provided that the Jewish Holocaust remains the ultimate crime that all of them unambiguously portend, much as scriptural antetypes anticipate their fulfillment. Intolerant Pilgrims killed Pequot Indians, a visitor to the Tolerance Museum will learn, and intolerant Germans would later kill Jews. The earlier crime was a portent of the definitive crime, since the Holocaust is the moral *terminus* toward which all of Western history was directed, the defining event which orientates everything that preceded it and everything that followed.

The Tolerance Museum—its Hebrew name is Beit Hashoah, House of the Shoah—teaches explicit Holocaust lessons that derive their power from the institutionalized elevation of Jewish wartime suffering into history's most horrible crime and from the concomitant moral obligation, now embedded in the educational system, to ensure that it never recurs, an obligation that requires continual instruction and continual self-inspection, as well as a systematic reevaluation of our history. All of us, Germans and non-Germans alike, must, if we follow the advice of the Simon Wiesenthal Center, self-police and combat our inner nazi, lest our racial prejudices metastasize into another Holocaust.

The USHMM on the Mall in Washington and the Museum of Tolerance in Los Angeles, along with all the other Holocaust memorials that litter the terrain between them, are physical embodiments of American Jewry's reinterpretation of the war, as well as public acknowledgments of its political triumph. The Jewish Holocaust is not a collection of German atrocities, real and fabricated; it is a racially aggressive broadening of culpability, a nazification of Western civilization relying on the normally unstated premise that the Allies were "just as guilty" as the Germans. It domesticates what was formerly an alien evil, ascribing to us the same pathology that we falsely ascribed to our enemy sixty years ago. The purgative confrontation with a criminal past that we once imposed on defeated Germans we now allow Jews to impose on ourselves.

SHOAH & HOLOCAUST

In its current Judeocentric meaning uncapitalized "holocaust" first tentatively entered English during the 1961 Eichmann trial in Jerusalem as a translation of Hebrew Shoah ("Disaster, Catastrophe"). Eichmann was accused of organizing this Shoah, the extermination of European Jewry, and American media coverage of the trial used "holocaust" as a rough English equivalent, following an existing Israeli practice.

Shoah, as a term designating the disaster that had befallen the Jews of Europe, had been in currency among Palestinian Jews even before the war, dating specifically to 1933, the year of Hitler's electoral victory in Germany, which was perceived as a disaster for Jews; and in 1942 enterprising Zionists in the *yishuv* had already begun plans for a memorial, later to become the Yad Vashem Holocaust Museum, to commemorate the Shoah, well before most of the deaths that the memorial would eventually memorialize had actually occurred. But outside of Israel Jewish deaths during World War II could not until the Eichmann trial be easily differentiated from the more than fifty million non-Jews who perished, and a "holocaust" remained a sacrificial burnt offering in its original biblical context, and a term denoting any destructive conflagration in everyday speech. In that latter sense "holocaust" had been used to describe various acts of destruction inflicted on the Allies by the Axis, with no implication that Jews were notable among the victims.

Before the dissemination throughout the West of *the* Holocaust, an exclusively Jewish holocaust categorically separate from other conflagrations, the suffering of European Jewry during the Second World War lacked a name and a distinct identity; it was just suffering, terminologically indistinguishable from other wartime suffering. The suffering of an American crippled on D-Day and the suffering of a Jew starved at Bergen-Belsen belonged to the same broad generic category of wartime suffering and wartime deaths. Both were violence inflicted on *us* by our common nazi enemy during the course of a terrible war which *we* had won.[17]

The Holocaust, capitalized to illuminate its earth-shaking import, was the deliberate disaggregation of Jewish dead from other Allied dead, with Jewish deaths receiving a special name and a special moral significance, forming a qualitatively distinctive wartime event, different in kind from all other wartime events and unprecedented in its world-historical implications. Hence the need for countless memorials to preserve its memory. Hence the need for educational prophylactic measures to prevent its recurrence. Hence the steadily declining significance of the war in which it occurred. World War II has now become, as Rabbi Berenbaum once boasted, a mere "background story" to the Jewish Holocaust.[18]

Yet the Holocaust, as it entered our vocabulary and our conceptual landscape in the 1960s and 1970s, was not simply Jewry's declaration of independence from the Allied victors; it also carried a judgment. With the arrival of the Holocaust, the nazi concentration camp, which had formerly testified to our comparative goodness, became the visible revelation of the vast moral failure of our entire civilization. "The guilt of Germany," Eliezer Berkovits

---

[17] On "Holocaust," see Novick, 20, 133–34; on "Shoah," see Segev, 434. Shoah commemoration was first proposed by Mordecai Shenhabi—the initiator of the memorial project that would later become Yad Vashem, Israel's most important Holocaust museum—as "a new cause that can turn into a pipeline for large sums." For Shenhabi and the early history of Yad Vashem, see Segev, 427ff. On the etymology and usage of "holocaust," see Appendix 2 below.

[18] *Washington Times*, January 10, 1991, quoted in "Rewriting History," *JHR* 14, no. 3 (May–June 1994), 44

proclaimed in 1973, "is the guilt of the West. The fall of Germany is the fall of the West. Not only six million Jews perished in the Holocaust. In it Western civilization lost its claim to dignity and respect."[19]

"The uniqueness of the Holocaust," the Zionist writer Gershon Mamlak explains, "was manifested in a dual form: the way the victims experienced it, and the way the Gentile world performed and/or witnessed it."[20] Mamlak offers a succinct statement of some important Holocaust dogmas. "Uniqueness" is crucial, providing a historiographic counterpart to the religious doctrine of Jehovah's selection of Israel as his preferred people. Jewish suffering

---

[19] Eliezer Berkovits, *Faith After the Holocaust,* 18. Cf. Marcia Sachs Littell, "Holocaust Education in the 21st Century," in *Proceedings of the Washington Conference on Holocaust-Era Assets* (Washington, DC: Government Printing Office, 1999), 874: "Merging Holocaust Studies into Jewish Studies is the wrong approach. It simply sends the wrong message. That the Holocaust is the most traumatic event in the death and life of the Jewish people since the destruction of the Second Temple goes without saying. But study of the Holocaust is also to study *the pathology of Western civilization* and its flawed structures. It must not be hidden away by false bracketing of courses" (emphasis added). Dr. Sachs Littell, a professional Holocaust pedagogue, is the director of the National Academy for Holocaust and Genocide Teacher Training. Her ideas for educating Euro-Americans about "the pathology of Western civilization" are in essence no different from the unvarnished hatred of Rabbi Dov Fischer, vice-president of the Zionist Organization of America: "We [Jews] remember that the food they [White Europeans] eat is grown from soil fertilized by 2,000 years of Jewish blood they have sprinkled onto it. Atavistic Jew-hatred lingers in the air into which the ashes rose from the crematoria" ("We're Right, the Whole World's Wrong," *Forward,* April 19, 2002).

[20] Gershon Mamlak, "The Holocaust: Commodity?," *Midstream* (April 1983), 12.

during the Second World War was different in kind from all other suffering, so unique that even comparing the Jewish Holocaust to lesser holocausts can be considered a form of blasphemy. Uniquely evil victimization should of course entail the unique evil of a specific set of victimizers, but in Holocaust discourse the Jewish victims of history's most unique crime stand in opposition to the whole Gentile world, which is conceptualized, in terms of its relation to the Holocaust, as a single category subsuming perpetrators and bystanders, each sharing a common guilt.

"The [non-Jewish] world," Rabbi Shlomo Riskin informed a group of Jewish tourists visiting Auschwitz, "is divided into two parts: those who actively participated with the Nazis and those who passively collaborated with them." German nazis and their allies murdered Jews; the entire Gentile world, comprised of active nazi participants and their passive collaborators, was culpable. Judaism's intense ethnocentrism has traditionally divided mankind into Jews and the "nations of the world," obliterating the differences that distinguish each non-Jewish nation from others, the defining feature of our various nations being, in Jewish eyes, their non-Jewishness and hence their inherent uncleanness. Holocaust discourse replicates that ancient division, not only tracing a line that divides Jews from everyone else but also erecting a moral barrier along the line, with all of us on the wrong side of it. "Over long centuries," according to Eliezer Berkovits, "especially in the Western world, the [Gentile] nations reacted to the existence of the Jewish people with a form of sadistic cruelty which to call beastly would be an insult to the animal world."[21]

---

[21] (Riskin) Tom Hundley, "Two Views of Horror," *Chicago Tribune*, May 9, 1993, quoted in Novick, 160; Berkovits, "Re-

Jerzy Kosinski's *The Painted Bird*, published in 1965 and set in wartime Poland, was among the earliest representations of the Jewish Holocaust's revelation of ubiquitous Gentile savagery, and it should be regarded as Diaspora Jewry's first significant literary expression of its emerging Holocaust consciousness. Kosinski's imaginative treatment of wartime horrors reflected a deliberate decision, like Miller's decision twenty years earlier, to define, with complete indifference to actual history, the generic White Other as the malevolent source of Jewish suffering, the modern Amalek. Kosinski (Lewinkopf) and his family were, as a matter of biographical fact, protected by Polish peasants during the brutal German occupation, but he nevertheless chose, when he came to pen his fictional Holocaust memoirs, to nazify his Catholic benefactors, transforming Poles into hate-filled pogromists who subject the novel's six-year-old protagonist to a series of fanciful sadistic cruelties, none of which ever occurred.

Kosinski's real-world experience in occupied Poland, a life of comparative comfort among the Poles he would later vilify, should have led him to endorse the victors' interpretation of the war: on one side evil Germans, on the other *us*, the evil Germans' enemies, in this case Poles and Jews. Nothing in that structure detracted from the uniqueness of the Jewish Holocaust; nothing in it would have limited Kosinski's artistic license. He was free to invent as many grotesque atrocities as his muse could inspire, so long as he attributed them to Germans, not Poles. Yet Kosinski chose instead, in a conscious act of racial aggression, to nazify the war's first anti-nazis, at the price of radically distorting his own experience.[22]

---

writing."

[22] Earlier Jewish literary interpretations of Nazi persecution generally aimed at inclusion. In Edward Lewis Wallant's

One purpose of the Eichmann trial had been, as Israeli Prime Minister David Ben-Gurion announced, to make the nations of the world feel ashamed. The trial was an exercise in mild nazification designed to suggest Allied

---

strange 1961 novel *The Pawnbroker*, the protagonist, a concentration camp survivor isolated from the world by his incommunicable experience of nazi savagery, is reintegrated into the human community through the empathic commiseration of a WASP woman named Marilyn and the redemptive sacrifice of a Puerto Rican named Jesus, an assimilationist thematic structure that later Jewish Holocaust writers would studiously avoid. The novel's uplifting conclusion, based on its heavily marked Christian symbolism, was largely excised in Sidney Lumet's 1964 film adaptation. Wallant's *Pawnbroker* has recognizable Holocaust themes (the radical isolation of survivors, the judaizing of the concentration camps, spectacular Nazi barbarity, etc.) but none of the political meanings that the institutionalized Holocaust would later express. *The Painted Bird*, on the other hand, is a true Holocaust novel with a Holocaust political structure, even though the nazi concentration camp is only tangential to its subject matter. For Kosinski's fabrications, see James Park Sloan, "Kosinski's War," *New Yorker*, 10 October 1994: "[Polish journalist] Joanna Siedlecka portrays the elder Kosinski [i.e. Jerzy Kosinski's father] not just as a wily survivor but as a man without scruples. She maintains that he may have collaborated with the Germans during the war and very likely did collaborate with the NKVD, after the liberation of Dabrowa by the Red Army, in sending to Siberia for minor infractions, such as hoarding, some of the very peasants who saved his family. Her real scorn, however, is reserved for the son, who turned his back on the family's saviors and vilified them, along with the entire Polish nation, in the eyes of the world. Indeed, the heart of Siedlecka's revelations is her depiction of the young Jerzy Kosinski spending the war years eating sausages and drinking cocoa—goods unavailable to the neighbors' children—in the safety of his house and yard."

co-responsibility for the Shoah while advertising the new Israeli refuge from eliminationist anti-Semitism abroad.[23] Zionist instrumentalizing of nazi persecution sought to encourage those Jews who only admired Israel from afar to enact Zionism, to dissolve the Diaspora by taking up residence in the Jewish state. Israel was an unassimilable people compelled for centuries to dwell apart as powerless exiles inside unappreciative nations; with the rebirth of territorial Israel Jews could return to their homeland, where they once again possessed the sovereign power to protect their apartness from its enemies. Kosinski's fabricated account of the nightmarish wanderings of an innocent refugee, threatened by Germans and tortured by psychopathic Poles, was ideologically congruent with Zionist political assumptions, which themselves expressed a common belief in the omnipresence of irrational Jew-hatred. But Zionism has always been halfway between a delusion and a lie: it is based on a sincere faith in Gentile malevolence, yet a faith not quite sincere enough to impel its adherents to remove themselves from the physical threat that Gentile malevolence theoretically poses. Kosinski himself left Poland for the United States in 1957, exchanging one exile (*galut*) for another, unwilling to avail himself of the refuge from further torments that reborn Israel offered.

Zionism proposed a resolution of the Jewish problem, which it frankly acknowledged, through the normalization of Jews within their own nation state. But when the Jewish ethnostate was finally achieved, most Jews felt no inclination, as Hitler had predicted in *Mein Kampf*, to ingather themselves *en masse* in Palestine, however much

---

[23] For the Zionist objectives behind the Eichmann trial, see Hannah Arendt, *Eichmann in Jerusalem: A Report on the Banality of Evil* (New York: Penguin, 1964), 5–10, and Segev, 327–28.

they cultivated a plaintive yearning to do so. The central Zionist message that motivated Israel's publicizing of the Shoah was irrelevant, almost a rebuke, to any Jew who chose to continue his now voluntary exile among the *goyim*, and the Shoah, as it incrementally took shape on American soil as the Holocaust, acquired a different purpose, at odds with the intentions of its Israeli promoters.

The Jewish problem, our perception of an alien race-nation existing within Western nations, could only be interpreted by immobile Diaspora Jewry as a symptom of the White problem—"racism," our desire to preserve our race-cultural integrity, a desire that could now be defined as a precondition for genocide. The resolution of the White problem has therefore been the principal objective of the Holocaust, which became an integral part of a campaign to eliminate the Jewish problem by declaring any perception of its existence pathological.[24] The Holocaust

---

[24] MacDonald documents this campaign in his *Culture of Critique*, esp. chapters 5–6. Cf. Raul Hilberg, *The Destruction of the European Jews: Revised and Definitive Edition* (New York: Holmes & Meier, 1985), 1044: "When in the early days of 1933 the first civil servant wrote the first definition of 'non-Aryan' into a civil service ordinance, the fate of European Jewry was sealed." Even if every word of the Holocaust story were true, Hilberg's pronouncement would remain obviously false. Its political purpose is, however, unmistakable. Racial classifications and definitions are routine in Israel, and it is unlikely that a single American Zionist has ever worried that they might lead to a Palestinian holocaust. As Arendt (*Eichmann in Jerusalem*, 7) noted: "In Israel . . . rabbinical law rules the personal status of Jewish citizens, with the result that no Jew can marry a non-Jew; marriages concluded abroad are recognized, but children of mixed marriages are legally bastards (children of Jewish parentage born out of wedlock are legitimate), and if one happens to have a non-Jewish mother he can neither be married nor

was absorbed into anti-racism, instrumentalized as its foremost political weapon for combating Eurocentrism and White racial cohesion. Sadistic nazi cruelties, far from demonstrating the need to end Jewish dispersion, instead supplied a new moral pretext for fragmenting Western nations in order to normalize Jewish self-selected otherness as one otherness in a sea of racial diversity. Contemporary Holocaust commemoration is in that respect a repudiation of Zionism, since it assumes the permanence of Jewish exile: Jews build Holocaust museums in the United States because they have no intention of leaving.

COLLECTIVE MEMORY

Diaspora Jews today remember their Holocaust and have convinced us that we should remember it as well, but in the years immediately after the war, when memory should have been most acute, they rarely spoke about nazi persecution and apparently forgot the painful trauma of European Jewry's wartime internment. Holocaust forgetting preceded Holocaust remembering. The murder of European Jews, the sociologist Nathan Glazer reported in 1957, "had remarkably slight effects on the inner life of American Jewry."[25] For about two decades after the liberation of the camps wartime suffering played an insignificant role in Jewish group thinking in the West, and the victors' interpretation of the war remained stable, largely

---

buried. . . . There certainly was something breathtaking in the naïveté with which the prosecution [in the Eichmann trial] denounced the infamous Nuremberg Laws of 1935, which had prohibited intermarriage and sexual intercourse between Jews and Germans. The better informed among the correspondents were well aware of the irony, but they did not mention it in their reports."

[25] Nathan Glazer, *American Judaism* (Chicago: University of Chicago Press, 1957), 114.

unchallenged by the Jewish revisionism that would eventually dethrone it.

In recent years various explanations for this phenomenon of Holocaust forgetting have been put forward, the most common being the psychoanalytic view that memories of attempted nazi genocide were far too painful to contemplate and were therefore repressed, just as survivors of child molestation are presumed to repress memories of their abuse. Whatever the reason, the fact remains, a fact conceded by everyone who has seriously examined the subject, that American Jews in the 1950s and early 1960s did not consider nazi persecution a central part of their group heritage. The Holocaust did not then exist as a discrete historical event and as a source of anti-racialist lessons, because Jews had not yet remembered it.

No new discoveries of old nazi evil prompted the collective decision of American Jews to shape their recovered memory of the camps into an indictment of the nations that liberated them. On the contrary: the Allies themselves were willing to believe, in the aftermath of the war, that nazis made lampshades from human skin, turned Jewish fat into soap, electrocuted Jews on conveyor belts, cultivated cabbages with Jewish fertilizer, and burned Jews alive in gas ovens. The Allies were willing, in other words, to attribute a much more lurid evil to their defeated German enemy than does contemporary Holocaust discourse, at least in its more scholarly forms. Yet postwar belief in unique, truly spectacular nazi evil did not generate the Jewish Holocaust.

The old heroic, pre-Holocaust view of World War II was valuable for Jews, and they had no legitimate reason to object to its particular set of lessons. In the postwar years anti-Semitism was driven safely to the periphery of American society. In a 1946 poll eighteen percent of Gentiles identified Jews as "a threat to America," which was myopically charitable; by 1954 the number had plummeted to one percent. Anti-Semitism, through its association with the defeated nazi enemy, had been delegitimized. "The fifteen or twenty years after the war," Novick writes, "saw the repudiation of anti-Semitic discourse and its virtual disappearance from the public realm." In the wake of NS Germany's defeat America became, in pronouncements by public figures, a "Judeo-Christian nation," since a national definition that failed to include our small Jewish minority implied nazi-like cultural homogeneity; in 1945 Bess Myerson became the first Jewish Miss America; in 1947 Hollywood's first treatment of anti-Semitism appeared, the overtly didactic *Gentleman's Agreement*, which Darryl Zanuck, the only major White film executive, campaigned hard to bring to the screen; and by the late 1950s the hagiographic treatments of Anne Frank—featuring (as novelist Cynthia Ozick has angrily complained) a deracinated, "all-American" Anne—had propelled her *Diary* into the canonical status it still enjoys today.[26] Jews, in short, were mainstream in postwar America, and anti-Semitism was not. The Holocaust was belatedly recollected in the near absence of the force its lessons were ostensibly intended to combat.

Postwar Holocaust forgetting is analytically significant. It allows us to see clearly that the Jewish Holocaust, regardless of the truth or falsity of its various factual claims, is an ideological construction dependent for its existence not on historical events in Europe but on contemporary political forces in America. A recovered memory that steadily grows more vivid and more impassioned as it becomes more distant is obviously much different from

---

[26] Novick, 113; Cynthia Ozick, "Who Owns Anne Frank?" *New Yorker*, October 6, 1997. On the *Diary* of Anne Frank, also see Appendix 3 below.

normal recollection. The idea of the Holocaust, apart from the facts and fictions that provide its raw material, has little to do with history, nor was it, as we have seen, an inevitable interpretation of the camps. The source of the Holocaust as an idea is located not in German concentration camps but in events within the United States in the 1960s, when American Jews first began, during the era of civil rights and counterculture, to vocally recollect memories of nazi persecution in Europe.

Jewish wartime suffering became the Holocaust, a discrete event to which uniqueness could be ascribed and for which Western civilization could be held responsible, at the very historical moment when racial victimization in the past began to confer political power in the present. The victors' interpretation of the war had provided important advantages in the 1950s, immunizing Jews from criticism and mainstreaming them within Euro-America; it provided fewer advantages in the 1960s, when a legacy of victimization became a moral bludgeon with which to extort political privileges from an increasingly besieged Euro-American majority.

The Holocaust was the Jewish brand of anti-White identity politics, an aggressive declaration of a distinctive Jewish identity based on *our* collective guilt for *their* unique suffering. The old view of the war had externalized evil in the nazi enemy; the Holocaust turned Jews into victims of unprecedented White violence, making the West itself the evil's source and rewarding Jews with their own special form of negritude. To number yourself among the wretched of the earth was a source of political power during the Black civil rights revolution, and it would be an even greater source of power in the decades that followed. Jews had played an instrumental role in fomenting the revolution, providing as much as three-quarters of the funding for civil rights organizations, and by tactically remembering the Holocaust they enlisted themselves among the minority groups eligible to profit from racial claims, while relieving themselves of membership, largely nominal in any case, in the White oppressor race, against which the revolution was and still is directed. Through the Holocaust the most successful ethnic group in American history not only joined the various aggrieved minorities staking out racial claims against White America, but also pushed itself to the front of the line.[27]

Jewish identity politics is, however, more than simple political calculation. There can be no doubt that the Holocaust is now genuinely central to Jewish group consciousness, as poll after poll reveals. "It's a sad fact," says Samuel Belzberg, a major financial supporter of the Tolerance Museum, "that Israel and Jewish education and all the other familiar buzzwords no longer seem to rally Jews behind the community. The Holocaust, though, works every time." Most Jews believe their own propaganda and they are often profoundly affected by it. "The Holocaust," the ADL's Abraham Foxman foolishly wrote in 1994, ". . . is not simply one example of genocide but a nearly successful attempt on the life of God's chosen children and, thus, on God himself."[28] Since such breathtaking ethno-

---

[27] Cf. "Farrakhan's Jewish Problem," *Tikkun* 9 (March–April 1994), 10, quoted in Novick, 191: "In current discourse, who gets labeled 'white' and who gets labeled 'person of color' derives not from the color of one's skin . . . but from the degree to which one has been a victim of Western colonialist oppression. By that measure, Jews have been the greatest victims of Western societies throughout the past two thousand years and must certainly be understood to be one of the 'peoples of color.'"

[28] (Belzberg) S. Teitelbaum and T. Waldman, "The Unorthodox Rabbi," *Los Angeles Times Magazine*, July 15, 1990, quoted in Mark Weber, "The Simon Wiesenthal Center," *JHR* 15, no. 4 (July–August 1995), 3; Abraham Foxman, "Schindler's List—

centrism endangers the necessary public fiction of the Holocaust's broad humanitarian meanings, it is safe to conclude that Foxman, the head of an activist Jewish organization teaching racial equality and human brotherhood, was allowing his real emotions to overcome his political judgment, an indication of an authentic psychological investment in unpluralist Holocaust lessons.

Peter Novick describes American Jewry's undeniable absorption in the Holocaust as a collective memory, a group perception of the past distinct from objective historical knowledge. A collective memory is formed in response to contemporary political and social needs, and it makes the implicit claim that the past, rather than being separated from us by the unbridgeable differences between now and then, remains a present reality expressing enduring truths about a group and its place in the world.

The Meaning of Spielberg's Film," ADL newsletter *On the Frontline* (January 1994), quoted in *JHR* 14, no. 2 (March–April 1994), 41. Sincere belief in the Jewish Holocaust does not of course preclude cynical exploitation of it. Cf. Novick, 157: "At a time [1981] when West Germany was considering the sale of arms to Saudi Arabia, [Hyman] Bookbinder wrote to the German ambassador to the United States in his capacity as a member of the U.S. Holocaust Memorial Council—though he was not, he made clear, speaking for the council. Plans for the Washington museum were now being developed, he said. 'How Germany will be treated in that museum may well be affected by the decision you make pertaining to the sale of arms to Saudi Arabia.'" Bookbinder believed that Gentile Holocaust consciousness was essential for preserving American "commitment to Israel," but for the sake of Israel the USHMM's presentation of Nazi atrocities was negotiable: the unique horrors of the Holocaust could become slightly less horrific if the West German government proved properly compliant.

A collective memory "suffuse[s] group consciousness," representing a group's identity both for itself and for others through a morally simplified construction that strips away distracting details and ambiguities in order to align history with contemporary group concerns. The Holocaust, according to Novick, is a Jewish collective memory, a reshaping of the past brought into present consciousness as a collective social mechanism for defining group identity.[29]

---

[29] On collective memory, see Novick, 3–6, 170ff. Novick, reflecting the consensus view, locates the principal source of awakened Holocaust memory in Jewish anxieties over Israel, prompted by the Six Day War of 1967 and especially by the Yom Kippur War of 1973. Cf. Marcia Sachs Littell, "Holocaust Education," 869-870: "In the years directly following liberation [of the camps] there was silence—stunning silence. From the Jewish Community, from the churches, from government agencies. During this time, the majority of Americans were comfortable with the silence. Even the word 'Holocaust' did not come into current use until the 1960s. . . . Americans received their first real jolt of awareness at the time of the Six Day War (1967) in Israel, when 'a Second Holocaust' seemed threatened. With the realization that Jews might be destroyed in their homeland, not only Jews in the Diaspora were aroused: Christians friendly to Jewish survival were also moved to act." But no explanation for the Jewish Holocaust that fails to acknowledge the racial hostility that animates it can be taken seriously. Elie Wiesel calls Auschwitz "the failure of two thousand years of Christian civilization" not because he supports Israel and fears for its survival, but because he hates the people he has chosen to live among and believes that he can now insult them with impunity. Holocaust memory had, in any case, clearly taken shape well before 1973 and even before 1967. There were already important (though lightly marked) Holocaust political themes in Stanley Kramer's *Judgment at Nuremberg* (1961), a "message picture" that gently suggested, for the

Put simply, the Jewish Holocaust is a racially self-interested belief about the past that tells Jews something about us and something about themselves that most deeply believe to be true. The Holocaust martyrology that we experience as propaganda, and must analyze as such, Jews have internalized as the central component of their racial identity.

Neal Sher, former nazi-hunter for the Office of Special Investigations, believes that "every Jew alive today is a Holocaust survivor," and each year on Yom Hashoah ("Shoah Day") Jewish students wear yellow stars to demonstrate their survivorship, a statement of racial identity that distinguishes them from us.[30] A group identity

---

educational benefit of British and American Gentiles, their own complicity in nazi evil; the nazification of Pope Pius XII, a process that continues today, began in the early 1960s, well before Diaspora Jews could possibly have felt any fears about an imminent holocaust in Israel; and "Holocaust theology," a now massive body of theopolitical scholarship centering all of human history in the Holocaust's various Judeocentric revelations, also precedes Israel's Six Day War. See Richard Rubenstein's seminal *After Auschwitz: Radical Theology and Contemporary Judaism* (New York: Bobbs-Merrill, 1966).

[30] *Jewish World* (Long Island), May 8–14, 1992, quoted in *JHR* 13, no. 1 (January–February 1993), 46. Sher, who left his job as a nazi-hunter to become Executive Director of the American Israel Public Affairs Committee (AIPAC), the chief Zionist lobby group in Washington, was speaking at a Yom Hashoah commemoration. The Brooklyn-born Dr. Baruch Goldstein, who in 1994 slaughtered twenty-nine Muslims praying in Hebron's Ibrahimi Mosque, often wore a yellow star, marked with the German "Jude" ("Jew"), in order to commemorate his particularist understanding of the Holocaust's moral lessons. Cf. Rubenstein, *After Auschwitz*, 153: "We stand in a cold, silent, unfeeling cosmos, unaided by any purposeful power beyond our own resources. After Auschwitz, what else can a Jew say about

modeled on the Holocaust survivor sanctions Jewish racial hostility by denying Jewish loyalty to anyone but themselves. The resistance fighter, celebrated in the old victors' narrative, was an active figure participating in a pan-European struggle of free men against fascist tyranny; the Holocaust survivor, Elie Wiesel being the most prominent example, is a passive object of cataclysmic violence at the hands of European civilization, a tragic victim whose unique experience of the literal hell that once took shape on earth makes him the bearer of ahistorical lessons about man's perennial inhumanity to Jews. The Holocaust survivor, abandoned to his fate and filled with a direct knowledge of metaphysical evil imparted by his incomparable suffering, stands as an indictment not only of Western civilization but often of a cruelly indifferent universe as well, and he has become the preeminent expression of Jewish collective memory, personifying a covertly belligerent restatement of Jewish apartness. Never have Jews been more openly welcomed by the Euro-American mainstream, yet never has their self-representation been more closely bound up in an embittered recollection of racial victimization.

Collective memory is a useful metaphor from a racialist perspective, since it highlights the real strangeness of American Holocaustomania, a guilt-ridden obsession with Jewish deaths that has gripped most of the Western world as well. If the Holocaust is, as Novick argues, the Jewish collective memory of World War II, then we who are not Jews are in effect thinking about our past with

---

God?"; Fackenheim, *Encounters Between Judaism and Modern Philosophy: A Preface to Future Jewish Thought* (Philadelphia: Jewish Publication Society, 1973), 166: "After the Holocaust, the Israeli nation has become collectively, what the survivor is individually."

someone else's memory, seeing both the past and its implications for the present through Jewish eyes rather than through our own. The Holocaust did not begin as our collective memory of the war. We have not shaped and simplified history into the Holocaust; Jews have, and their memory has become ours. Thus we now think we see Jewish Holocaust survivors, rather than anti-nazi dissidents and European resistance fighters, in photographs of Buchenwald and Dachau, our old political interpretation of the camps having been displaced and forgotten. And thus, much more importantly, we now think we were responsible for the Holocaust and have allowed Jews to erect permanent monuments wherein, under their direction, the guilt many of us readily acknowledge is publicly commemorated.

There can be no mystery how the Jewish Holocaust became our collective memory, the retrospective propaganda with which we also envision the Second World War. Our Holocaust memory is the result of Jewish power, especially media power. In the Jewish-owned *New York Times*, as Finkelstein notes, the only subject that receives more coverage than the Holocaust is the weather. Jews have dominated Hollywood from its inception, and by the 1960s, the decade of the Holocaust's invention, they were substantially overrepresented in all the various professions that disseminate culture. Jews, that is, create many of the thoughts with which we think. Jews also control the American mass media, and have done so for at least forty years, so they wield the crucial propaganda instruments, enabled by low levels of anti-Semitism, that can transform their thoughts into our public opinion. In 1965 they could turn Kosinski's nazification of the Poles into an instant classic; in 1945 they did not yet possess either the power or the confidence to so elevate Miller's *Focus*. On this general issue of Jewish power Novick is frank: "We [Jews] are not only 'the people of the book,' but the people of the Hollywood film and the television miniseries, of the magazine article and the newspaper column, of the comic book and the academic symposium. When a high level of concern with the Holocaust became widespread in American Jewry, it was, given the important role that Jews play in American media and opinion-making elites, not only natural, but virtually inevitable that it would spread through the culture at large."[31]

A FRAGILE VICTORY

The Holocaust must be numbered among Jewry's most impressive victories in their new hunting grounds, second only to the 1965 liberalization of immigration law, which opened American borders to the Third World. There are now Holocaust memorials in most major American cities, as there are in almost all Western capitals, and we are in the midst of a deluge of Holocaust remembering in films and books and on television that shows no signs of subsiding. There are numerous Holocaust Studies programs in universities, staffed by professional Holocaustologists who owe their livelihoods to the further propagation of Holocaust lore, and Holocaust education flourishes in the public schools, drawing us ever closer to the full integration of anti-racialist Holocaust instruction into school systems across the country, the stated ambition of the President's Holocaust Commission, the USHMM's forerunner.

---

[31] Novick, 12. Novick (207) comments further: "A good part of the answer is the fact—not less a fact because anti-Semites turn it into a grievance—that Jews play an important and influential role in Hollywood, the television industry, and the newspaper, magazine, and book publishing worlds. Anyone who would explain the massive attention the Holocaust has received in these media in recent years without reference to that fact is being naive or disingenuous."

All these various forms of Holocaust commemoration teach political lessons that Jews want us to learn. A well-indoctrinated Euro-American who has internalized the lessons of the Jewish Holocaust will not object to non-European immigration into the United States; a Jew who has internalized the same shared collective memory will acquire a more emotional commitment to his racially exclusive *Heimat* in Palestine. Therein lies, of course, the danger of thinking with someone else's thoughts. Holocaust commemoration racializes Jews and deracializes Whites; it strengthens them and weakens us.

But we can question whether this victory will persist. Holocaust memory, because it took shape in the virtual absence of anti-Semitism, projects deep Jewish hostility that otherwise would have remained better concealed. It is compelled, by both the political purposes and the group psychology that brought it into existence, to disparage non-Jews: "the world owes Jews" only if the world as a whole is guilty of grievous offenses against Jews. A view of history that of necessity says something good about Jews but bad about almost everyone else is inherently fragile and liable to provoke resentment. Henry Kissinger opposed the construction of the USHMM, fearing that aggressive Holocaust commemoration would provoke anti-Semitism, and he might have been correct. The victors' narrative exiled Germany from civilized humanity while celebrating the heroics of White fratricide; the Holocaust nazifies any assertion of White national consciousness, even in nations with distinguished anti-nazi credentials, thus constructing and potentially unifying its own opposition. National patriotism and belief in the Jewish narrative of horrifically unique persecution are increasingly incompatible, and the descendants of both the winners and the losers of the Second World War have a common interest in repudiating the old mythology of nazi evil, since it has become an ideological weapon against all of us, providing anti-national justification for a host of globalist policies ranging from Third World immigration to NATO's "humanitarian bombing" of the now nazified Serbs, whose wartime heroism we once rightly applauded.

The Holocaust also suffers from dangerous contradictions. Jews have the power to transform their preferred ideas into our public opinion, but they cannot control the direction in which the ideas subsequently migrate. Alongside the hard Holocaust lessons of White guilt are the soft Holocaust lessons of human brotherhood, which are indispensable to the Holocaust's marketing strategy in the Diaspora as well as formal elements in its multicultural agenda. The survival of the Jewish ethnostate evidently requires daily violation of these humanitarian ideals of tolerance and racial pacificism, which their promoters in the Diaspora never had any intention of imposing on their far-flung brethren but now increasingly find arrayed against the only nation for which they feel any genuine loyalty.

Contemporary anti-Zionism is a species of anti-racism, and anti-racialist Holocaust lessons therefore hand anti-Zionism new weapons. Palestinian collective memory tactically calls Arab dispossession in 1948 the *Naqba* ("Disaster"), a name and an idea clearly modeled on the Zionist Shoah. The competing postcolonial narrative of Palestinian racial victimization, with its calculated nazification of Israel's origins, dominated the 2001 UN Conference on Racism at Durban, where Third World delegates relabeled Zionism as racism and angrily denounced Israeli genocide. For Israel the universalist lessons of the Holocaust are poor camouflage, only revealing Zionism's systematic rejection of the anti-racialism that Jews so aggressively promote everywhere else. The militant Left in the United

States and the bulk of liberal opinion in Europe have now abandoned the Jewish state, condemning it as a colonialist project founded on ethnic cleansing and sustained by apartheid. In Israel's ongoing war against brown-skinned Arabs there can be no doubt which side more closely resembles the potent propaganda image of the Nazi. Anti-racialist ideas that effectively serve Jewish interests in the Diaspora become toxic when applied to Israel, and no number of additional Holocaust museums will alter that fact.

Jewish success in propagating such an unstable ideological construction, thereby provoking opposition from nationalists on the Right while strengthening anti-Zionism on the Left, may yet prove a Pyrrhic victory. Holocaust commemoration winnows out friends until only enemies remain, and Jews risk finding themselves alone against the world.

APPENDIX 1:
ON THE ETHNIC COMPOSITION
OF CONCENTRATION CAMP INMATES

For the racial composition of the camps liberated by Americans, see Novick, 65, 295n.8. Josef Kramer, commandant of Bergen-Belsen, where Anne Frank succumbed to typhus, told British liberators that his camp's internees were "habitual criminals, felons, and homosexuals," which was inaccurate, but more accurate than the now dominant judaizing interpretation that makes every camp survivor an inoffensive Jew. Many of the earliest accounts of wartime internment were written by non-Jews, because the nazi concentration camp had not yet become exclusive Jewish cultural property. For a critical discussion of early camp literature, see Paul Rassinier, *The Holocaust Story and the Lies of Ulysses* (Costa Mesa, Cal.: IHR, 1978), where the ethnic demography of the internees is evident.

As Novick pointedly notes, the relative scarcity of Jews in the camps liberated by Americans did not prevent Holocaust industrialist Deborah Lipstadt (author of *Denying the Holocaust*) from spotting malicious anti-Semitism in the failure of press coverage to mention Jewish internees with sufficient frequency. It would be hard to find a more succinctly illustrative example of Holocaust scholarship, which is essentially an aggressive scrounging for sources of racial grievance. Lipstadt was, of course, engaged in her own small-scale nazification of the liberators.

A concentration camp, regardless of its actual demographics, has retroactively become holy Jewish soil, and belligerent Jews will characterize as racial hatred any failure to specify its exclusive owners. Cf. Cynthia Ozick, "The Rights of History and the Rights of Imagination," *Commentary* 105, no. 3 (March 1999), 27: "How is it possible for a writer to set forth as a purposeful embodiment of the inmost meaning of the camps any emblem other than a Jewish emblem? It is possible the way it is possible to plant crosses, with heated [i.e. 'racist, hateful'] intent, over the soil of Auschwitz."

This passionate belief in exclusive Jewish ownership of the concentration camp is a product of current Jewish identity politics and constitutes a rejection of earlier interpretations of the war. In *Memory of the Camps*, a British propaganda film containing the dramatic documentary footage of Bergen-Belsen, the narrator (actor Trevor Howard) carefully practices a literal ecumenicism in his description of the assembled corpses: "And so they lie—Jews, Lutherans, and Catholics, indistinguishable, cheek-to-cheek in a common grave." Similarly for Dachau: "Here were 32,000 men of every European nationality, including 5,660 Germans." Leon Uris, in his militantly Zionist *Exodus* (New York: Bantam, 1958), an unapologetic celebration of Jewish apartness in ethnically cleansed Israel, retained (with no "heated intent") the same broad inclusion even in his account of the genesis of Auschwitz: "In addition to Jews to dispose of there were Russian, French, and other prisoners of war, partisans, political enemies in occupied countries, religious fanatics, especially Christians of the Catholic faith, gypsies, criminals, Freemasons, Marxists, Bolsheviks, and Germans who talked peace, liberalism, trade unionism, or defeatism. There were suspected foreign agents, prostitutes, homosexuals, and many other undesirable elements. All these had to be eliminated to make Europe a fit place for Aryans to live" (133–34). Few Holocaust pedagogues practice such (admittedly comical) inclusion today.

The USHMM rigorously excludes non-Jewish victims, despite an explicit mandate to the contrary, and when Americans liberate a Dachau satellite in an episode ("Why We Fight") of Spielberg's HBO miniseries *Band of Brothers* (2001), the "others" that Uris so carefully listed as targets of nazi mass murder have vanished, leaving only Jews with yellow stars. As an unparalleled racial crime against Jews, the Jewish Holocaust has no tolerance for White Gentiles distorting its symmetry, and it therefore prefers to annihilate them from memory. The USHMM-sanctioned Liberators Project, a notorious fabrication in which Black soldiers liberate Jews from Buchenwald and Dachau, thus had the advantage, from a Jewish perspective, of eliminating White Gentiles not only from the inmates of the camps but also from their liberators, thereby constructing liberation as a symbolic episode in the history of anti-racism. See Mark Weber and Greg Raven, "Multi-Media 'Liberators' Project Exposed as Fraud," *JHR* 13, no. 3 (May–June 1993), 4.

APPENDIX 2:
THE ETYMOLOGY AND USAGE OF "HOLOCAUST"

Etymologically "holocaust" ("completely burned") derives from the Septuagint, the Greek version of the Old Testament, where *holokauston* translates Hebrew *holah* ("that which goes up"). A "holocaust" (e.g. Leviticus 1.3-17, Judges 6.26-28, 1 Samuel 7.9) was a burnt offering (Gk. *holos* = wholly; *kaustos* = burned), usually an unblemished male animal sacrificed to Jehovah, to whom its smoke "went up." The biblical origin of the term is, however, immaterial to its initial deployment, although the religious connotations of a "holocaust," together with the prevalence of smoke and fire in some Holocaust writing, may have facilitated the later sacralization of Jewish deaths.

Israeli attorney general Gideon Hausner, Eichmann's Polish-born prosecutor, used "holocaust" (for Shoah) in English-language media interviews, and during and especially after the trial lowercase "holocaust" gradually became common in discussions of nazi persecution, following the word's standard nonbiblical meaning ("consuming conflagration, wholesale destruction"). Elie Wiesel did not (as Holocaust scholarship, assisted by Wiesel's own inaccurate memory, often assumes) first apply "holocaust" to nazi genocide in 1963. Cf. Oscar Handlin, "Jewish Resistance to the Nazis," *Commentary* 34, no. 5 (November 1962), 401: "The holocaust . . . was a product not of the Jewish response or of the Jewish situation, but rather of the powerful engine of destruction the Germans controlled—a bureaucracy of uniquely remorseless and irresistible efficiency." In Handlin's usage "holocaust" means "massive (racial) destruction," thus "genocide"; but although he may have felt a Jewish proprietary interest in the term, in 1962 "holocaust" could still easily be applied to non-Jewish deaths and non-German perpetrators, with no risk of trespassing on Jewish cultural property. Handlin's holocaust was not precisely "the Holocaust," since the latter had not yet come into full conceptual existence in the West.

Two years later Alfred Alvarez, in a survey of "The Literature of the Holocaust" (*Commentary* 38, no. 5 [November 1964], 65–69), discussed the concentration camps in largely ecumenical terms as "symbols of our own in-turned nihilism" and "a focus of contemporary suffering," with the suggestion that they might prove a mere "small-scale trial run for a nuclear war." (In American usage of the early 1960s, "holocaust" referred commonly to "nuclear holocaust.") For Alvarez, a noted literary critic writing in an official Jewish publication, "the holocaust" (still uncapitalized) was a distinct event but not a distinctly Jewish event, a convenient opportunity for erudite philosophizing about the traumas of modernity rather than a source of racial grievance or anti-Western polemics.

Earlier in the same year Emil Fackenheim could still write "On the Eclipse of God" (*Commentary*, 37, no. 6 [June 1964], 55–60) without mentioning the holocaust or nazi persecution, briefly adducing only unspecified "catastrophes" that imperiled religious belief; by the end of the decade Fackenheim had become (along with Eliezer Berkovits and Richard Rubenstein) a founder of Holocaust theology, busily explicating "the commanding voice of Auschwitz," his new vocation devoted to rhetorically outdoing coworkers in discovering bold new formulations of the Holocaust's cataclysmic significance. See "Jewish Values in the Post-Holocaust Future: A Symposium," *Judaism* 16, no. 3 (Summer 1967), 266–99, and Fackenheim, *God's Presence in History: Jewish Affirmations and Philosophical Reflections* (New York: New York University Press, 1970).

The Holocaust, as the powerful propaganda construction we experience today, began coalescing around 1965 with the publication of Alexander Donat's family memoir *The Holocaust Kingdom,* a phrase which other Jewish writers (including Fackenheim) soon adopted. In the years that followed "Holocaust," now often capitalized and preceded by the definite article, appeared in a growing body of essays and books authored by Jews, who by the late 1960s were asserting their ownership of the term and feeling a strong political interest in its further propagation. Nora Levin's *The Holocaust* appeared in 1968, and in the same year the Library of Congress adopted "Holocaust, Jewish (1939–1945)" as a Judeocentric rubric for titles that had previously been listed under headings like "World War, 1939–1945 — Jews." In the early 1960s Jewish writers had sometimes spoken of "Hitler's holocaust" in order to distinguish their holocaust from other holocausts (e.g. Edwin Samuel, "One for Six Million," *Saturday Review,* 18 May 1963); by the beginning of the next decade such clarification seldom seemed necessary.

The 1978 NBC miniseries *Holocaust,* by far the most influential popularization of Judeocentric wartime history, placed capitalized "Holocaust" firmly in American consciousness as (in Elie Wiesel's words) "the Event," a distinctly Jewish tragedy of unparalleled magnitude; but that carefully orchestrated propaganda triumph only solidified a semantic invention that had been effected several years earlier, namely the creation of *"the* Holocaust," a superholocaust which does not simply tower above other holocausts but actually reduces them to mere comparisons. Since the early 1970s anyone speaking of an uncapitalized, non-Jewish "holocaust" (e.g. "an ecological holocaust," "the Ukrainian holocaust," or even "a nuclear holocaust") has understood that the word properly belongs to the Jews and that he is only briefly borrowing it to suggest a similarity, an analogical practice now regularly denounced by belligerent Jews as lexical theft.

APPENDIX 3:
ON THE DIARY OF ANNE FRANK

Jewish hostility to the popular stage (1955) and film (1959) adaptations of Anne's *Diary*, both written by the White husband-and-wife screenwriting team of Albert and Frances Hackett, has become strident in recent years, a result of Holocaust consciousness and modern Jewish identity politics colliding with an established monument of wartime patriotism.

In "Who Owns Anne Frank?" (*New Yorker*, October 6, 1997) Cynthia Ozick, an especially volatile Zionist, argues that it would have been better if the Diary had been burned before publication, to prevent it from teaching anodyne, dejudaized lessons about Jewish suffering mediated through the moral universalism of non-Jews. Ozick and others import into Anne Frank's life a strong Jewish consciousness she never possessed, while bizarrely blaming Gentiles (along with Anne's "deracinated" father) for having disfigured her into a WASP in all but birth, a pallid symbol of the Jew as merely one of us.

In fact current Jewish anger at the broadly faithful film version, which Jews in the 1950s justifiably considered a remarkable propaganda triumph, reveals growing frustration with Anne and the heroic version of the war she honorably embraced, frustration so great that some Holocaust pedagogues recommend ejecting her from the canon of Holocaust authors for teaching insufficiently Judeocentric lessons; but because her *Diary* has become a quasi-religious document, scrutinized for its spiritual insights as fundamentalist Christians pore over their Bibles, belligerent Jews generally direct their attack against White America, which in the 1950s allegedly betrayed the text for malevolently assimilationist purposes, an example of what Ozick calls "them stealing our Holocaust." Accordingly in

Holocaust education programs White students now not only read Anne Frank's *Diary of a Young Girl*, but also learn about the Eurocentric act of cultural theft that once misappropriated it from its rightful owners. The falsely rejudaized *Diary*, surrounded by polemical commentary, becomes in the process a Holocaust text with a Holocaust political structure.

For summaries of the Jewish culture war over the *Diary*, an emotional intramural dispute barely comprehensible to any non-Jew, see Novick, 117–20; Molly Magid Hoagland, "Anne Frank, On and Off Broadway," *Commentary* 105, no. 3 (March 1998), 58-63; and Ian Buruma, "The Afterlife of Anne Frank," *New York Review of Books*, February 19, 1998.

http://library.flawlesslogic.com/holocaust.htm

A different version of the preceding essay was published as "Holocaust Commemoration, Part I: Lessons in Tolerance," *National Vanguard*, no. 124, October–November 2004, pp. 26–31, and "Holocaust Commemoration, Part II: Metamorphosis of an Idea," *National Vanguard*, no. 125, January–February 2005, pp. 8–9, 20–30.

Remembering the Holocaust

Holocaust Guilt

We are now all so familiar with Holocaust rhetoric from Jewish organizations that its characteristic audacity can easily pass unnoticed:

> When Jews feel and say that Germany and those in Europe who supported, or at least did not oppose the Nazi regime, should never be allowed to forget, events back them up. — Anti-Defamation League's *Letter From Europe*, July 2000.

The number of Germans and other Europeans who "supported . . . the Nazi regime" is by now very small; more than a half-century has passed since Adolf Hitler's death. So the ADL do not mean, despite the literal sense of the sentence quoted above, that Jews will never allow eighty-year-old Germans to forget their support for National Socialism sixty years ago; nearly all will be dead within the decade. They really mean young Germans — and young Lithuanians, young Croats, young Italians, young Finns etc. The nations themselves, they are saying, should never be allowed to forget, and Jewish organizations like the ADL plan to make their collective guilt for Nazism a permanent feature of their national identities.

That much should be obvious. Perhaps it even makes sense. Nations often feel collective pride in their ancestors' achievements; perhaps they should also feel collective shame for their ancestors' crimes.

But there is an additional, very large group that finds itself included in the ADL's program for punitive Holocaust remembering: "those in Europe who . . . did not oppose the Nazi regime." The ADL are, again obviously, not concerned about eighty-year-old Spaniards or eighty-year-old Swedes or eighty-year-old Swiss "who . . . did not oppose the Nazi regime." Nor do they mean a French housewife who, sixty years ago, neglected to rescue Jews from the clutches of the German occupiers. The ADL mean young Frenchmen and young Spaniards and young Swedes and young Swiss. They, too, must always remember.

So you are guilty and must never be allowed to forget, nor should your children be allowed to forget, if your grandfather "supported the Nazi regime"; you are also guilty and must never be allowed to forget, and your children should never be allowed to forget, if your grandfather merely failed to "oppose the Nazi regime." Not opposing Hitler and supporting Hitler incur the same guilt and the same obligation to remember. That means that most Europeans and their children must never be allowed to forget the Holocaust, and the ADL assume not only their own ability to speak, but also their power to ensure that others listen. If Jews want twenty-year-old Swedes and their children never to forget, their remembering is certain.

What if your grandfather did, in fact, oppose the Nazi regime? You might at least think that twenty-year-old Americans or Englishmen would be under no obligation to remember perpetually the Holocaust. But if that idle thought briefly crossed your mind, you were mistaken. Mandatory Holocaust remembering is almost as pervasive in the United States and Great Britain, nations that fought to destroy National Socialism, as in the nation where it was born.

That European Jews were killed not only by Germans but also by "apathy" and "silence" in the United States and Great Britain, the apathy and silence being products of an ingrained "anti-Semitism" that the Anglo-American world shared with its German enemies, is now a standard teaching of Holocaust lore, which treats inaction and collaboration as crude synonyms. The failure of the Allies to bomb rail lines leading to Auschwitz, now the subject of a $40 billion lawsuit by Jewish "survivors" against American taxpayers, is the preferred example of this inaction/collaboration; the failure of the Western democracies to rescue Jews on the *St. Louis*—a failure also, though rarely mentioned, of the Jewish Agency in Palestine—is another popular complaint. The West, all Holocaust promoters agree, either killed Jews in, or failed to rescue Jews from, history's most horrible crime, so the West as a whole stands condemned by both its acts and its inaction, with a mere handful of Righteous Gentiles, the vast majority being decidedly unrighteous, providing rare exceptions that only prove the rule.

"The free and 'civilized' world," Elie Wiesel claims, handed "[the Jews] over to the executioner. There were the killers—the murderers—and there were those who remained silent." Wiesel invokes here the newly minted crimes of "indifference" and "abandonment," which Jewish Holocaust promoters have manufactured in order to add the former heroes of World War II to its cast of villains, almost as guilty as the Germans they fought. Nazis and anti-Nazis are conflated, by their shared guilt, into a single category, the former for their crimes against Jews, the latter for their sinful indifference to the crimes. "The Jews of Europe," Jewish historian Irving Abella writes, "were not so much trapped in a whirlwind of systematic mass murder as they were abandoned to it."

The simple truth, of course, is that Jewish organizations and Jewish historians and Jewish "survivors" want every White Gentile to feel guilt for the Holocaust, so they have invented a series of *ad hoc* excuses for broadening the class of the "guilty" to include all of us, whatever our grandfathers were doing sixty years ago.

THE HOLOCAUST INDUSTRY

One of the undeniable strengths of *The Holocaust Industry: Reflections on the Exploitation of Jewish Suffering* (London: Verso, 2000), Norman Finkelstein's often furious denunciation of rapacious Holocaust profiteering, is its demystification, for a mainstream audience, of all this Holocaust lore as nothing more than an instrument of "Jewish aggrandizement" wielded for both political power and profit. The Holocaust industry of the title is a network of Jewish historians and Jewish institutions that exploits the Holocaust in order to acquire the diverse political benefits that a history of victimhood now offers, in addition to the very substantial pecuniary rewards that Jewish organizations have successfully squeezed from European governments and corporations in what Finkelstein calls "an outright extortion racket."

Holocaust "scholarship" and Holocaust "memory," themselves often funded from the racket's proceeds, are seldom, Finkelstein argues, disinterested historical investigations or politically innocent recollections of Jewish suffering, as their practitioners would have us believe, but are instead expressions of an ideological structure that serves current political interests, principally the Jewish *Heimat* in Palestine and its Zionist supporters in the United States. German atrocities against Jews are the Holocaust industry's raw material, ethnically self-serving propaganda its finished product.

Prof. Finkelstein identifies two central ideas underlying the Holocaust industry's omnipresent propaganda: "(1) The Holocaust marks a categorically unique historical event; (2) The Holocaust marks the climax of an irrational, eternal Gentile hatred of Jews." The former he dismisses as "intellectually barren and morally discreditable," the latter as a simple fiction, popular among Jews but transparently false. Both dogmas are, however, mutually self-sustaining and jointly they construct a radically ethnocentric world-view, with the Holocaust at its center. Jews are distinguished from everyone else by virtue of their historical moment of unparalleled suffering, and Gentiles are distinguished from Jews by having nurtured the hatreds that culminated in this moment of unparalleled suffering. Jews were victims of history's greatest crime, and they have been, over millennia, the objects of the perennial Gentile hatred that eventually caused history's greatest crime. The entirety of non-Jewish history is therefore indicted. At any moment the unique evil of the Holocaust could have occurred, the hatreds that caused it being perennial, and since the hatreds are entirely irrational, with no relation to antecedent Jewish behavior, Jews bear no responsibility for having in any way provoked them. "For two thousand years," Elie Wiesel believes, ". . . we were always threatened. . . . For what? For no reason."

The political benefits of Holocaust dogmas are substantial. Cynthia Ozick can explain hostility to Israel by denying the need for an explanation: "The world wants to wipe out the Jews . . . the world has always wanted to wipe out the Jews." The incommensurate evil of the Holocaust also offers an esthetically compelling symmetry. Thus Leni Yahil, in her unapologetically Zionist study of *The Holocaust*, on the establishment of the Jewish State: "Destruction unparalleled in history was contrasted with a creation unparalleled in history." Anyone who has seen *Schindler's List* should be familiar with the symmetry: From the black-and-white darkness of the Holocaust European Jewry emerges into the bright colors of its own Jewish State. And if, as Wiesel says, Auschwitz represents "the failure of two thousand years of Christian civilization," then each escalation of the preeminent evil that Auschwitz now signifies is an additional indictment of Christian civilization and an additional justification for a Jewish State physically separate from it. Zionists therefore have an interest in maintaining Holocaust dogmas and in ensuring their dissemination, since the Holocaust helps immunize Jews against criticism in the Diaspora, where they form a vulnerable minority among potentially genocidal majorities, and inhibits criticism of Israel, which serves a permanent refuge for Jews should eliminationist anti-Semites once again attempt unparalleled destruction.

The monetary benefits of Holocaust dogmas are also substantial. Finkelstein's case against Holocash extortion, the core of his book, is detailed and devastating. No one who has read *The Holocaust Industry* could fail to find unintended humor in Abraham Foxman's recent claim that Jewish organizations regard the collection of Holocaust reparations as a "sacred mission." Some highlights:

❖ Holocaust profiteers wildly exaggerated the value of dormant accounts in Swiss banks, the subject of a massive Jewish campaign of national vilification directed against Switzerland, including the fraudulent claim that the banks robbed Jews of as much as $20 billion. Of the $1.25 billion eventually paid by the Swiss to the World Jewish Congress (WJC), at most only $200 million were genuinely owing, and contradicting the repeated claims of Jewish organizations, the independent Volcker Committee found no evidence that Swiss banks mishandled dormant Jewish accounts.

❖ Holocaust profiteers, in this case the Simon Wiesenthal Center, falsely charged, in order to assist the extortion racket, that the Swiss interned Jewish refugees in "slave labor camps" during the war. The historical record is clear: They didn't.

❖ Holocaust profiteers, the WJC and the World Jewish Restitution Organization, have formally agreed to exclude Israeli banks from their extortion campaign, even though they also hold dormant Holocaust-era accounts. Finkelstein comments: "The writ of these Jewish organizations thus runs to Switzerland but not to the Jewish state." Further: "The most sensational charge leveled against the Swiss banks was that they required death certificates from the heirs of Nazi Holocaust victims. Israeli banks have also demanded such documentation. One searches in vain, however, for denunciations of the 'perfidious Israelis.'"

❖ Holocaust profiteers launched their recent campaign for compensation in the name of "needy survivors," but most of the money that they have thus far extorted is destined for the coffers of Jewish organizations and will be spent to fund more Holocaust education and Holocaust memorials and Holocaust studies, like much of the more than $61 billion in reparations already paid by Germany prior to the current round of extortion. Tellingly, "survivors" themselves, familiar with the institutional greed of their self-appointed spokesmen, prefer to be paid directly by the German government.

❖ Holocaust profiteer Edgar Bronfman, head of the WJC, "movingly testified before the House

Banking Committee that the Swiss should not 'be allowed to make a profit from the ashes of the Holocaust.' On the other hand, Bronfman recently acknowledged that the WJC treasury has amassed no less than 'roughly $7 billion' in compensation monies."

❖ Holocaust profiteers have regularly inflated the number of Jewish "slave laborers" in order to extort additional money from European corporations. And since each increase in the number of Jewish "slave laborers" alive today logically requires a corresponding decrease in the number of Jews who died in German concentration camps, the Holocaust industry is practicing its own mercenary version of "Holocaust denial." If Jewish claims for compensation are correct, then the Holy Six Million figure must be false. Finkelstein quotes his mother, herself interned at Majdanek: "If everyone who claims to be a survivor actually is one, who did Hitler kill?" Or as David Irving once put it: "Another Holocaust victim is born every day."

❖ Holocaust profiteers falsely claimed that former "slave laborers" never received compensation from Germany, although they were "covered under the original agreements with Germany compensating concentration-camp inmates" and have received payments amounting to the equivalent of $1 billion in contemporary currency. "Still, 50 years later the Holocaust industry was demanding money for 'needy Holocaust victims' who had been living in poverty because Germans allegedly never compensated them."

❖ Holocaust profiteer Elie Wiesel demands a minimum lecture fee of $25,000, as well as a chauffeured limousine.

Finkelstein concludes: "The current campaign of the Holocaust industry to extort money from Europe in the name of 'needy Holocaust victims' has shrunk the moral stature of their martyrdom to that of a Monte Carlo casino."

Although most prominent ideologies have, for good or ill, been subjected from the anti-Western Left to analyses of the political interests they serve, the Jewish Holocaust, which now looms over a host of what should be entirely unrelated subjects, has hitherto been exempt, largely as a result of the Holocaust industry's successful campaign to theologize Jewish suffering, transforming it from concrete events at a particular time into an ahistorical object of religious reverence, replete with taboos that few outside the Racial Right dare violate. Finkelstein's marked lack of deference to conventional Holocaust pieties and the rules of Holocaust correctness intentionally desacralizes the Holocaust in order to deprive its exploiters of the aura of sanctity that shields their schemes from scrutiny, and in this objective he shares something in common with the revisionist Robert Faurisson, who has debunked "the religion of the Holocaust" for more than two decades. Yet tactical taboo violation does not demonstrate disbelief in the religion of which the taboos form a part. Finkelstein, as we shall see, shares the faith and therefore objects to those who would abuse it. But many of his Holocaust convictions are indistinguishable from those of the Holocaust industry he attacks, and his "radical" critique of Holocaust orthodoxy ends up restating some of its most important dogmas in an only marginally less pernicious form.

There is an obvious lesson in this. If as a society we delegate to Jews, as in effect we have done, the job of explaining criticism of Jews, we should not be surprised that the answers they arrive at have little to do with themselves and much to do with us. The most popular of their answers—that the source of anti-Semitism is our irrational hate—was predictable before the investigation ever began, given the ethnic composition of the class of experts eligible to conduct it. Similarly, if in mainstream discourse the charge of anti-Semitism remains so devastating that only Jews can safely attack Holocash extortion, we can anticipate that Jewish biases may affect the character of the attack, given the practical impossibility of anyone other than a Jew launching it. There is much of value in *The Holocaust Industry*, but much also that reflects an internal ethnic squabble among Jews in which, predictably, crucial Holocaust premises remain uncontested.

DISCOVERING THE HOLOCAUST

Once upon a time, not so long ago, the suffering of European Jewry during the Second World War lacked a name. It was just suffering. The suffering of an American soldier crippled on D-Day, the suffering of a Jew starved at Bergen-Belsen, and the suffering of a German woman crucified on a barn door all belonged to the same broad generic category of wartime deaths and wartime suffering. In the Western democracies historians and the public at large paid, naturally enough, more attention to first two than to the latter, more attention to *our* suffering than to theirs, but no one believed that *ours* deserved a special name.

Beginning in the 1960s, during the course of the Civil Rights Revolution, that changed. One group, until then numbered on *our* side, the Jews, began to distinguish their suffering from everyone else's. Jews in Israel had, in fact, already defined their wartime suffering as distinctively un-Gentile by assigning it a special Hebrew name, and with remarkable forethought the Jewish National Fund in pre-Zionist Palestine had already started plans, in 1942, for a memorial to this "Shoah" ("Catastrophe"), later to become the Yad Vashem Museum, before most of the events it would memorialize had actually occurred. But in the Diaspora Jewish suffering, correctly or not, was still only suffering, and Jewish deaths, from among the more than fifty million who died during the war, were still only deaths.

"Holocaust," the English version of "Shoah," was first deployed to describe distinctively Jewish suffering during the 1961 Eichmann trial in Jerusalem, a trial consciously conducted as an educational enterprise, and it was not until the late 1960s that "Holocaust" began its ascent into public consciousness in the English-speaking world, propelled by a steadily growing number of essays and books bearing the term, most authored by Jews. In 1968 the Library of Congress replaced "World War, 1939–1945—Jews" with "Holocaust, Jewish (1939–1945)"; in 1978 the influential television mini-series *Holocaust* appeared, watched by almost a hundred million Americans, its advertising financed by Jewish organizations; and in the same year President Carter established a commission, chaired by professional "survivor" Elie Wiesel, to create a national museum in Washington memorializing Jewish suffering in Europe.

Holocaust remembering accelerated rapidly in the decade that followed, and by 1991 Rabbi Michael Berenbaum, then project director of the Holocaust Memorial Museum, could boast, accurately, that World War II was merely a "background story" to the Holocaust. The contrary view, that the Holocaust was a footnote ("point de détail") to the war, is now illegal in France and much of Europe, as the French nationalist leader Jean-Marie Le Pen discovered. The old view of World War II has not only been supplanted; in some countries it has literally been criminalized.

The Jewish Holocaust was a run-of-the-mill horror in a century that saw many horrors, no worse than the Armenian holocaust, or the Cambodian holocaust, or the Russian holocaust, or the Rwandan holocaust, or the Ukrainian holocaust, and arguably no worse, at the level of individual suffering, than the Palestinian *Naqba*; if any of us had a choice between spending eight months in Auschwitz, the duration of Elie Wiesel's internment, or fifty years in a Palestinian refugee camp, only a fool would choose the latter. Whose suffering gets publicly commemorated is a political decision based not on the magnitude of the suffering but on the political lessons that the commemorators hope to privilege. Different suffering teaches different lessons. The Jewish Holocaust can plausibly teach the dangers of race-cultural self-assertion on the part of majorities and the attendant moral obligation to respect minority differences. The Ukrainian holocaust could plausibly teach much different lessons: the murderous results of internationalist attempts to eradicate national loyalties, as well as the hatred that a certain unassimilated minority often feels for its host populations. Everyone has heard of Adolf Eichmann and almost no one has heard of Lazar Kaganovich because as a society we judge the first set of lessons preferable to the second.

There should be no real mystery why this occurred. Holocaust education in the public schools, Holocaust Studies programs at most major universities, a Week of Holocaust Remembrance in mid-April, annual Holocaust commemorations in fifty states, a Holocaust Museum on the Washington Mall, Holocaust documentary after Holocaust documentary, Holocaust film after Holocaust film—

all testify either to the absolutely unprecedented character of Jewish suffering during World War II, a suffering that dwarfs all pseudo-holocausts into pitiable insignificance, or else to the power of Jews to foist their racial agenda on White Gentiles. Since the first alternative should be unthinkable—the death-tolls of Soviet and Chinese Marxism were twenty million and sixty-five million respectively, according to the *Black Book*—no one can seriously discuss contemporary "Holocaust mania" without also discussing Jewish power.

Finkelstein has, however, no intention of discussing Jewish power, and he resolves the problem, in his own mind, by recourse to a fantasy common across the mainstream political spectrum, from Rush Limbaugh on the Right to Noam Chomsky on the Left—the fantasy of Israel as a valuable strategic resource, "a proxy for US power in the Middle East" necessary to ensure cheap oil and docile Muslims. Because the Holocaust deflects legitimate criticism of the Jewish State, Finkelstein argues, incessant remembering of the Holocaust also serves American foreign-policy objectives.

It is difficult even to conceive how this Israeli proxy is supposed to function, and there is no evidence that it does function, witness the price of oil, a devastating oil embargo in the 1970s, and the conspicuously undocile Muslim terrorists who now regularly attack Americans. But the proxy's phantom existence enables Finkelstein and some others on the Left to identify their anti-Zionism as a species of anti-Americanism. Leftist criticism of Israel becomes *de facto* criticism of American geopolitical objectives. The latter are, Finkelstein imagines, really responsible for the billions shipped annually to Israel, and Zionist lobby groups in Washington, motivated not by distinctively Jewish group loyalty but by the raceless pursuit their own political agendas, are only the willing facilitators, "marching in lock-step with American power." The unexamined assumption—that support for Israel benefits the United States—remains unexamined. No one need discuss Jewish power, Finkelstein has convinced himself, because Jewish power is only a useful tool in the hands of much more powerful non-Jewish "ruling elites." America's apparently Israel-first Middle East policy, far from indicating the ability of Jewish lobby groups to distort the democratic political process for their own ethnocentric purposes, as an unexpert could easily delude himself into believing, actually reflects the opposite, the absence of any significant, racially self-interested Jewish power. Zionist Jews still must remain beholden to their Gentile wire-pullers.

Finkelstein accordingly locates the beginning of frantic Holocaust remembering precisely in June of 1967, when American Jewry and the non-Jewish ruling elites who control U.S. foreign policy first recognized the geostrategic value of Israel, in the wake of the Jewish State's unexpected victory over its Arab neighbors. Jewish elites became "the natural interlocutors for America's newest strategic asset," a role that offered them access to real political power, until then denied to Jews. They would abandon Israel and the Holocaust propaganda that helps sustain it the moment that Israel ceased to be, in the eyes of their Gentile benefactors, a valuable surrogate for Imperial America, since their Zionism and their awakened Holocaust memory are not the result of racial emotions, but only of unsentimental political calculation.

The argument cannot be taken seriously, but absent clairvoyant insights into the minds of the amorphous Jewish elites Finkelstein alludes to, it would be hard to disprove. We can only say that it does not adequately explain actual Jewish behavior. Why, for example, would Jewish elites, in this instance namable elites, repeatedly agitate for the release of Jonathan Pollard? They derive no political benefit from it, and they run the considerable political risk of irritating non-Jews, most of whom still regard treason as a serious offense. The simplest answer is the most convincing: Pollard is a Jew who spied on non-Jews for the benefit of the Jewish State, and Jewish elites feel racial loyalty toward him both as a fellow Jew and as an Israeli spy. They are therefore willing to take political risks, with no hope of political benefits, to secure his release.

Or consider the example of Neal Sher, former "nazi-hunter" for the Office of Special Investigations, later head of AIPAC, the chief Zionist lobby group in Washington. When Sher declares that "every Jew alive today is a Holocaust survivor," the commonsense assumption that he is asserting, comically but nevertheless with complete sincerity, his emotional solidarity with the Holocaust's Jewish victims plausibly accounts for both his former profession and the ruthlessness with which he and his fellow Jewish "nazi-hunters" have pursued it: deporting octogenarians to face Communist kangaroo courts during the Cold War, arranging tragi-comic trials in which senile alleged "war criminals" testify incoherently from their hospital beds, illegally suppressing exculpatory evidence in the Demjanjuk case, threatening impoverished East European countries with economic penalties, and so forth. Again the political risks are real, as Jews visibly exploit Gentile institutions to exact racial vengeance on their enemies from a half-century ago. Give the devil his due: The hatreds of Sher and his ilk are genuine, not tactical.

Most Diaspora Jews, as their actual behavior plainly demonstrates, do have a strong emotional attachment to their Jewish State, and most also have a strong emotional attachment to their politicized interpretation of the Holocaust. Finkelstein's implausible thesis was necessary, from his perspective, only because the fact, if openly acknowledged, of strong Jewish racial loyalties will inevitably lead anyone who thinks seriously about the political abuse of the Holocaust to anti-Semitic conclusions. Incessant Holocaust promotion by Jews has some obvious ulterior motives, none of which has anything to do with American foreign-policy objectives: to delegitimize nationalism within majority-White nations; to legitimize Jewish nationalism in the Jewish State; to immunize Jews from criticism; to extract money from Germany, the United States, Switzerland, etc. Holocaust remembering is, in short, part of a racially self-interested agenda—it helps Jews and hurts us.

THE LESSONS OF THE HOLOCAUST

The Jewish Holocaust, we are told endlessly, teaches universal "lessons," and there are now taxpayer-funded Holocaust museums throughout the West, along with an extensive miseducational apparatus, designed to impart these supposedly crucial "lessons," applicable (so we are instructed) to everyone everywhere. But the principal "lesson" that the Holocaust teaches is, undoubtedly, the lethal consequences of any racial or national consciousness among Whites. Because White racialism and intolerance and nationalism led to the Holocaust, White racialism and intolerance and nationalism must be eradicated, to avoid future holocausts. In terms of practical politics a politician who opposes Third World immigration on racial or even on cultural grounds has failed to learn the "lessons of the Holocaust"; the largely successful Jewish campaigns to tag Patrick Buchanan and Jörg Haider with the "Nazi" label/libel are recent cases in point.

The Holocaust Museum in Washington announced its anti-White objectives early on, even before its construction: "This museum belongs at the center of American life because America, as a democratic civilization, is the enemy of racism and its ultimate expression, genocide." Genocide is, according to Jewish Holocaust lore, the natural outcome of any racial self-assertion by people of European descent, and American democracy is, by Jewish fiat, devoted to the extirpation of every vestige of our racial consciousness. That, not surprisingly, is what organized Jewry has wanted all along, as Kevin MacDonald has thoroughly documented.

In theory, the "lessons of the Holocaust" should teach Jews that Israel cannot ethically remain an explicitly Jewish state, committed to the preservation and advancement of a single *Volk*, rooted in land, tradition and blood, but must instead become a multiracial "state of its citizens," bound together only by abstract political principles and an eagerness to celebrate diversity, like the nationless anti-nations most Diaspora Jews now demand that their host populations become. In practice, needless to say, few Jews and no major Jewish organizations allow logical consistency and the lessons of the Holocaust to interfere with their racial self-interest. On the contrary: "The heart of every *authentic* response to the Holocaust," writes philosopher Emil Fackenheim, ". . . is a commitment to the autonomy and security of the State of Israel." Whereas in Israel Jews have formed a Jewish State for themselves and permit no one but Jews to immigrate into it, not even the Palestinian Arabs they ejected in 1948, in the Diaspora they campaign for multiculturalism and Third World immigration. Jews hate all nationalisms save their own; they are nationalists within Israel, but anti-nationalists everywhere else.

Broad Jewish support for Zionism in Israel, coupled with strident opposition to any form of racialism or nationalism in the Diaspora, is the defining hypocrisy of contemporary Jewry. Finkelstein, like the late Israel Shahak, is not guilty of it. He is a principled man: He opposes racialism in the United States, so he also opposes it in Israel. Yet he is apparently unaware of, or unwilling to acknowledge, his own anti-racialist debt to the "shelves upon shelves of [Holocaust] schlock" under whose weight American libraries are currently groaning. What has been, beyond any doubt, the most politically significant lesson of the Holocaust, the evil of White "racism," is almost completely absent from his text, appearing only in two sentences in the final chapter:

> Seen through the lens of Auschwitz, what previously was taken for granted — for example, bigotry — no longer can be. In fact, it was the Nazi Holocaust that discredited the scientific racism that was so pervasive a feature of American intellectual life before World War II.

Auschwitz did not, of course, scientifically discredit scientific racism, but it is certainly true that the academic study of racial differences has been discredited by its association with German National Socialism, although the facts themselves remain indifferent to the lessons of the Holocaust. It is also true that "bigotry is no longer taken for granted," but this bland summary of the sea-change in post-war attitudes to race requires a translation. Finkelstein, like most multiracialists, believes that the majority-White nations of the West are still riddled, from top to bottom, with bigotry and systemic "racism." The fight against White "racism" has scarcely begun; the lessons of the Holocaust have only taught us that bigotry should no longer be taken for granted.

An unwillingness to acknowledge their own impressive victories is a common characteristic of anti-White ideologues. The near absence of American borders does not inhibit Chicano activists from angrily denouncing the alleged "racism" of the small remnant that remains; the presence of a massive system of mandated racial discrimination directed against Whites does not inhibit "civil rights" activists from angrily denouncing (statistically nonexistent) "institutional racism" allegedly directed against Blacks. Anti-racialist campaigns need a perpetual state of emergency to eliminate the cultural toxin of "racism," but the scarcity of the toxin only escalates demands for more emergency measures. Demands for further Euro-American capitulation are invariably presented as though no significant capitulation has yet occurred. Whites have foolishly divested themselves of their former racial consciousness, but they receive no credit for their new racelessness, only more vilification.

Thus in the midst of a culture soaked in White guilt, Finkelstein recommends more of the same, while presenting his proposals as part of a radical assault on a conservative Holocaust Establishment too timid to berate the *goyim* with the severity they deserve. "We could," he says, "learn much about ourselves from the Nazi experience," and he helpfully suggests additional atrocities that we might, if so inclined, also commemorate: European "genocide" in the Americas; American atrocities during the Vietnam War; American enslavement of Blacks; murderous Belgian exploitation of the Congo. All of these suggestions for atrocity commemoration have a feature in common that should not be too difficult to discern, and with the likely exception of the last, each could be dutifully recited by any well-indoctrinated schoolboy, thanks to multicultural miseducation.

Finkelstein has further suggestions. We could also contemplate, while learning much about ourselves from the Nazi experience, how "Manifest Destiny anticipated nearly all the ideological and programmatic elements of Hitler's *Lebensraum* policy"; how German eugenics programs, commonly regarded as precursors of the Jewish Holocaust, merely followed American precedents; how the Nuremberg Laws were a milder variant of the Southern prohibition of miscegenation; how "the vaunted Western tradition is deeply implicated in Nazism as well," Plato and Rousseau being the proto-Nazis Finkelstein has in mind. Clearly, learning from the Nazi experience means learning to see the Nazi in ourselves and in our history.

Here Finkelstein's self-described radical critique of Holocaust orthodoxies has a parasitical relation to what it purports to debunk, tacitly relying on alleged Holocaust uniqueness in order construct a tenuous guilt-by-association which would be laughable in any other context. Hitler opposed "birth control on the ground that it preempts natural selection"; Rousseau said something similar. Most American states once had eugenics laws sanctioning the sterilization of mental defectives; the Nazis had similar laws. Leo Strauss called this form of nonreasoning the *reductio ad Hitlerum*. We are expected to see, and unfortunately most Whites will indeed see, not discrete ethical issues but a sinister pattern that establishes culpability. Yet the sinister pattern of culpability only exists if the Holocaust remains, on account of its unparalleled evil, the *terminus* toward which all of Western history was directed; the pattern ceases to exist if the Holocaust is dislodged from its position high atop a hierarchy of suffering. Substitute the Judeo-Bolshevik slaughter of Ukrainians for the Jewish Holocaust and you will also select a different set of signposts leading to a different unparalleled evil.

Since Finkelstein does not practice what he preaches, avoiding the implications of his own call to democratize suffering, his preferred Holocaust lessons turn out, as we have seen, to be not much different from the anti-racialist lessons that Holocaust promoters already teach. Elie Wiesel would have no objection to most of Finkelstein's pedagogy of White guilt, though he would of course insist that Jews need not be among its pupils. White guilt is a given for both; they differ only on how we should best commemorate it and on whether Jews should be included among the group to whom the requisite lessons must be addressed. We are, Finkelstein and Wiesel agree, morally obliged to "confront" and "remember" Nazi crimes, even though the confronting and remembering will be "difficult" and "painful," because we were somehow complicit in them, and in this both articulate what is now surely the core dogma of Holocaust propaganda. "[To] study ... the Holocaust," says Marcia Sachs Littell, director of the National Academy for Holocaust and Genocide Teacher Training, "is also to study the pathology of Western civilization and its flawed structures." Rabbi Eliezer Berkovits, Holocaust theologian, goes further: "The guilt of Germany is the guilt of the West. The fall of Germany is the fall of the West. Not only six million Jews perished in the Holocaust. In it Western civilization lost its claim to dignity and respect."

Such expressions of anti-Western animus, routine in Jewish Holocaust writing, would be very difficult to reconcile with Finkelstein's account of the genesis of Holocaust remembering, namely that organized Jewry "forgot" the Holocaust throughout the 1950s and then, in order to become valued participants in American statecraft, tactically "remembered" it in 1967, so that "Jews now stood on the front lines defending America—indeed, 'Western civilization'—against the retrograde Arab hordes." Anti-Western animus is, on the other hand, very easy to explain within the socio-political context of the decade when, by all accounts, the Holocaust received its English name and began its ascent into popular consciousness. American Jewry's decision to remember the Holocaust was dependent on White America's willingness to listen. A speaker normally presupposes an auditor, and vocal Holocaust remembering likewise presupposes receptive Holocaust listening. Jews had no intention in the 1960s, and they have no intention now, of remembering their Holocaust in the absence of a non-Jewish audience.

American Jews conveniently recovered their forgotten Holocaust memory at the very historical moment when racial victimization in the past began to confer political power in the present. Since Jews are more intelligent and much more politically powerful than other aggrieved minorities, they have elevated their wartime victimization above all other victimizations, while surrounding it with a deceptive, often eloquent language of humane universalism. The Jewish victims of the Holocaust, philosopher Paul Ricoeur writes, are "delegates to our memory of all the victims of history," a formulation which in practice means that all of history's other victims can be safely ignored or consigned to a small, dark corner in your local Holocaust museum, being somehow included in the representative suffering of the Jews. Thus this exceptional piece of Holocaust lore from Yad Vashem's Avner Shalev: "We add our voice to those who believe that the Holocaust, because of its Jewish specificity, should serve as a model in the global fight against the dangers of racism, anti-Semitism, ethnic hatred and genocide." The sentence is logically incoherent but its meaning is clear: Jewish specificity ensures universality. And the political subtext is also clear: In the holy war against "racism," one race of victims is far more equal than the rest.

JEWISH SELF-SEGREGATION

In the famous film footage of the liberation of Bergen-

Belsen, a British soldier, a kind of Everyman Tommy, states the Allied consensus at the time: "When you actually see a place like this ... you know what we are fighting for." Surveying the same evidence, General Ira Eaker, of the United States Eighth Air Force, drew a similar conclusion: "Let any doubter, in all the generations to come, contemplate what it would be like to live in a world dominated by Hitler, the Japanese warlords, or any other cruel dictator or despot."

Neither the British soldier nor General Eaker saw in the corpses of Belsen the pathology of our vaunted Western civilization, or the consequences of American eugenics laws and *Lebensraum* policies, or (in Wiesel's words) the "shameful legacy" of pre-war immigration quotas, or the moral imperative to celebrate racial diversity. Neither would have accepted any of the preceding even if a helpful "Holocaust educator" had patiently explained them all; neither would have understood what the "Holocaust educator" was talking about. *We*, the civilized democracies, had just defeated *them*, the cruel dictatorships. Belsen and the other camps showed conclusively what *we* had just saved the world from. The average Mississippi Klansman would have concurred.

There were serious errors in this triumphalist vision of the war. A cruel despot, in fact history's cruelest despot, Joseph Stalin, had been the main beneficiary, and the Red Army, even as the British soldier was speaking, were in the process of liberating Eastern Europe in the name of Soviet Marxism, raping and murdering as they liberated. A war that had nominally begun to prevent a historically German city, Danzig, from rejoining the German Reich, as most of its citizens wanted, had ended with not only Danzig but all of Eastern Europe in the hands of the Communists. And Belsen itself, which supplies our visual impressions of what the Holocaust "looked like," happens to be among the German concentration camps that most clearly fit the revisionist thesis: that the bulk of deaths in the camps, and the emaciated bodies that form the Holocaust's compelling iconography, were the result not of a program of deliberate extermination but of dislocations, caused by Allied bombing, in the final months of the war.

But the triumphalist consensus was culturally benign, at least for those nations that had fought on the winning side. It said something good about ourselves, and it dignified the many lives that the war had needlessly cost. The consensus should have served Jewish interests as well. Anti-Semitism was a distinctive vice of the cruel German dictatorship that the democratic Allies had just defeated, and it was therefore delegitimized, just as fascism and national socialism were delegitimized. Significantly, the first two Hollywood films attacking anti-Semitism, *Crossfire* and *Gentleman's Agreement*, both appeared in 1947, the latter receiving an Academy Award for Best Picture. The war's aftermath offered a didactic opportunity to define anti-Semitism as incompatible with the West's highest ideals, which Allied soldiers had supposedly shed their blood defending. With Hitler's defeat the enemies of the Jews were placed outside our Civilization, which should have encouraged Jews to curtail their frequent efforts to subvert it.

The Jewish group decision to shape their Holocaust memory into an indictment of Western "anti-Semitism" and "racism" — our "pathology" — was a calculated repudiation of post-war triumphalism. The Jewish Holocaust, as it emerged from the burgeoning identity politics of the 1960s, blurred and even effaced what had formerly been a clear distinction between *them* and *us*, cruel dictatorships and civilized democracies, and it set Jewry apart from both. There were now, in Wiesel's analysis, "murderers" and "those who remained silent" on one side, and innocent Jews on the other, a much different binary opposition that allows no place for the exploits of the formerly heroic Allies. The corollary of this intense ethnocentrism is the doctrine of the world's criminal "abandonment" of the Jews, a doctrine that distinguishes Jews from everyone else, to the detriment of the latter. "The world," we recall, "has always wanted to wipe out the Jews," which is another way of saying that Jews owe loyalty to nobody but themselves.

The alleged "pathology of Western civilization," with the Holocaust as its foremost symptom, has been constructed incrementally by a series of choices in which Jews, Norman Finkelstein among them, have broadened what was previously the specific evil of the Nazis into the general evil of the West, so that, as German historian Ernst Nolte puts it, "*Homo hitlerensis* ultimately appears as merely a special case of *Homo occidentalis*." Just as Jews are representative victims, so all Euro-folk, assuming the role once assigned to Germans alone, are representative perpetrators. *We*, including the descendants of World War II's victors, are now potential Nazis who are capable, if not for anti-racialist training and regular visits to Holocaust museums, of repeating uniquely evil Nazi crimes. Unique Nazi evil has been expanded to include all of us, without suffering any diminution in the process.

Teaching the lessons of White guilt has been a longstanding mission of Jewish propagandists. The potential Nazi lurking behind the conventional American hero was the barely concealed subject of *Crossfire*, which introduced to the screen a radically new character who would be immediately recognized by a modern audience, the pathological White hate criminal, in this case a superficially normal veteran, a police officer before the war, who gratuitously murders a Jew; Dore Schary, producer of *Crossfire*, later became the national chairman of the ADL, thus making a seamless personal transition from cultural to explicitly political Jewish activism. *Crossfire* was an early attempt to "learn much about ourselves from the Nazi experience," and contrary to Finkelstein, there is no shortage of such educational opportunities today. Recent Holocaust promoters, emboldened by our current affection for racial self-flagellation, have simply ascribed to Western man in general the pathology which their less ambitious forebears confined to lone madmen.

Insofar as we accept, as far too many of us do, the false moral burden to feel racial guilt over ("learn much about ourselves from") German wartime atrocities, real and fictional, we have internalized Jewish ethnocentrism, learning to see ourselves through Jewish eyes. We should therefore learn our own "lesson of the Holocaust" — that the descendants of both the winners and the losers of the Second World War now have a common interest in repudiating the old mythology of unique Nazi evil, along with the anti-Western Holocaust industry which has fastened itself on it.

http://library.flawlesslogic.com/industry.htm

Spielberg & the Eleven Million

"The Holocaust has increasingly become, for the democratic world at least, a symbol of all the other Genocides, for racism, anti-Semitism, hatred of foreigners, ethnic cleansing, and mass destruction of humans by humans generally. The reason for this is, possibly, that a vague realization is taking hold of people that the Holocaust, the planned total annihilation of the Jewish people at the hands of the Nazi regime, is both a Genocide like other Genocides, and also an unprecedented event in human history, which should serve as a warning to all of us."

—Prof. Yehuda Bauer, Yad Vashem

In an episode of Steven Spielberg's miniseries *Band of Brothers* (2001) American soldiers, the men of Easy Company, stumble upon a German concentration camp, a satellite of Dachau, where to their horror they discover hundreds of emaciated Jews, along with about an equal number of Jewish corpses. It is the spring of 1945 and we are—or so Spielberg would have us believe—in the midst of an extermination facility, one part of the vast industrialized machinery of mass murder designed to effect the nazi Final Solution, the physical extermination of the Jewish people. All of the inmates in the camp are thus Jews, identified by the yellow stars stitched into their striped camp uniforms, and they identify themselves as Jews to the startled liberators.

That was Spielberg's first inaccuracy, which we shall call Falsehood #1. Most of the inmates at Dachau and Buchenwald, about eighty percent, were non-Jews. When we look at photographs of liberated German concentration camps, we now think that all of the "survivors" we see are Jews. But that, as a matter of uncontested fact, is untrue. In 1945 American media coverage of the liberation of the camps on German soil rarely spoke of Jews, for the simple reason that Jews were a minority among their various inmates. The Americans who liberated the camps did not "confront the (Jewish) Holocaust," as Spielberg's *Band of Brothers* wants us to assume. They instead discovered, as a contemporary British documentary put it, "men of every European nationality, including ... Germans."

Falsehood #1 — the ejection of Gentiles from Dachau and their replacement with Jews — generates a problem for Spielberg. If all of the inmates in the concentration camp presented in *Band of Brothers* are Jews, and if Hitler wanted to exterminate all Jews, then why are the inmates still alive? That is also, of course, the monumental problem that the Jewish Holocaust has always faced. Why did the Germans fail to kill all the Jews under their control? Why did they bother to evacuate Jewish internees from the East? Why is Elie Wiesel, evacuated in 1945 from Auschwitz in Poland to Buchenwald in Germany, still alive? Why was Anne Frank not gassed at Auschwitz? Why was she instead relocated to Bergen-Belsen, where she tragically succumbed to typhus?

By falsely making all of his camp's inmates Jews, Spielberg faces the same problem, and he invents a solution — Falsehood #2. The camp guards, a Jewish survivor tells Spielberg's American liberators, desperately shot as many of the inmates as they could, knowing that the imminent arrival of Allied liberators would end their genocidal mission. Then they ran out of ammunition. So they fled, no doubt disappointed at their failure to implement fully their part of the Final Solution to the Jewish Question. They had killed as many Jews as they were able to kill, but not as many Jews as they had wanted to kill (i.e., all of them, every single person in the camp). The emaciated Jews we see on the screen are still alive because the nazi killers fortuitously ran out of bullets.

Even for most mainstream Holocaust scholarship, the presence of survivors at Dachau poses no insurmountable problem, since the bulk of the inmates interned there were not Jewish. We should keep that significant yet often overlooked fact in mind: In 1945 none of the American liberators of German concentration camps believed that they had uncovered the physical machinery of a plan to murder all Jews, because the majority by far of the inmates they liberated were Gentiles. A mainstream historian today can account for living men and women in Dachau even if he accepts the proposition that NS Germany planned the extermination of all Jews.

Falsehood #1, which amounts to the judaizing of Dachau, is necessary for Spielberg, because it preserves the concentration camp as distinctively Jewish symbolic territory. Spielberg, who rediscovered his Jewishness after studying the Holocaust, has no intention of commemorating German crimes by depicting non-Jews as the majority of the victims. He wants to retain the potently Jewish symbolism of a concentration camp, established in public consciousness by hundreds of Holocaust films and Holocaust memorials, and he is willing to ignore factual history to achieve his political aims. Falsehood #2—the claim that Germans tried to exterminate Dachau's inmates—is also necessary for Spielberg, because without it the death camp presented on our television screens would be reduced to an internment camp or even to a mere prison, ceasing to appear as a site for genocide. A nazi concentration camp not dedicated to genocidal mass killing would be a contradiction in terms.

We are thus prepared for Falsehood #3, which is the

ideological culmination of the others. A final notice, which brings this episode of *Band of Brothers* to its conclusion, reads: "During the following months, Allied Forces discovered numerous POW, concentration, and death camps. These camps were part of the Nazi attempt to effect the 'Final Solution' to the 'Jewish Question.' Between 1942 and 1945 five million ethnic minorities and six million Jews were murdered — many of them in the camps."

Falsehood #3 — the "five million ethnic minorities" — is more complex than its two predecessors and requires a longer explanation.

In popular memory the Holocaust is the extermination of Six Million Jews. Any man on the street asked to put a numerical figure to the Holocaust's victims will have a simple answer: Six Million. Yet at a more official level the Holocaust is really the extermination of Eleven Million: Six Million Jews plus five million "others," even though those "others" are generally absent from the Holocaust's public representations. Many Holocaust museums, including the US Holocaust Memorial Museum (USHMM) in Washington, are officially dedicated to the Eleven Million.

Unsurprisingly the Jews running the USHMM have blithely ignored an explicit mandate to that effect, secure in the knowledge that no politician would dare complain that the Museum is too Jewish and should diversify itself by sharing almost half its space with five million dead Gentiles. In theory, however, about half of the Holocaust is non-Jewish, and if the Holocaust were an affirmative-action employer, about half of all the Holocaust films and Holocaust museums and Holocaust educational programs would be devoted to non-Jews.

In *Band of Brothers* Spielberg elects, as an act of multicultural inclusion, to present the Holocaust as the extermination of the Eleven Million, not simply of the Six Million, because he wants to construct Dachau as an unmistakable embodiment of "racism." He wants us to believe that Germans murdered, in camps like Dachau and elsewhere, Six Million Jews and five million other minorities as part of their deranged racial vision of the world, which required the physical extermination of various non-optimal racial types, not only Jews. The liberation episode in *Band of Brothers* is thus appropriately entitled "Why We Fight," indicating that the Americans who liberated the camps belatedly discovered an "anti-racist" justification for World War II in their horrific "confrontation with the Holocaust." A White American in 1940 might not have known what "racism" could lead to—he might even have been a "racist" himself—but after he saw "racism" concretized in the camps in 1945, he knew what he had been unwittingly fighting to prevent. That, at any rate, is the lesson Spielberg hopes we will learn.

This formally inclusive anti-racism also provides an official rationale for the presence of the USHMM on the Mall in Washington, at the symbolic heart of American nationhood: "This museum belongs at the center of American life because America, as a democratic civilization, is the enemy of racism and its ultimate expression, genocide." The Eleven Million are a more ecumenical and democratic statement of anti-racism than the Six Million, and they imply that not only Jews have a stake in the institutionalized commemoration of Jewish deaths. The five million others are always dispensible, but they are, despite their virtual absence from public view, structurally useful to the Holocaust when it provides anti-racist lessons to multiracial America, because they prove that Holocaust commemoration is not simply a self-serving warning against the evils of anti-Semitism. If you think of yourself as a racial or an ethnic minority, then you too are included in the Holocaust, even though you may find yourself relegated to a few footnotes or (as in this case) to a single line at the conclusion of a television program that has otherwise deliberately excluded you.

Spielberg could have accomplished his educational objective by eliminating Falsehood #1 while retaining Falsehood #2. In other words, he could have visibly embodied the Eleven Million in a throng of emaciated European "ethnic minorities" milling about the camp awaiting liberation, with a few Jews wearing yellow stars sprinkled among them. Falsehood #2 could have been spoken by (say) a Pole or a Serb, a non-Jewish minority, a member of one of the ethnic groups whose victims (allegedly) comprise the five million.

Although Polish Holocaust survivors in speaking roles are likely too WASPish for the purposes of contemporary anti-racism, and although Jews hate Poles even more than they hate Germans, their visible presence would be a reasonable concession to the historical fact that most of the inmates at Dachau were Gentiles, many of them Poles and Catholics. *Band of Brothers* would have remained, even with this gesture to multiethnic inclusion, an ideologically driven fiction, still falsely presenting Dachau as a place where Germans warehoused minorities whom they planned (when time and available ammunition permitted) to murder; yet it would have been spared the burden of one theoretically unnecessary lie, the lie that Dachau was filled with Jews.

Spielberg is not, however, interested in anti-racism alone, so the lie was politically imperative. He, like most Holocaust promoters, has little interest in generic anti-racism. He prefers a special kind of anti-racism, a Judeocentric anti-racism wherein his Jewish minority can stand for other minorities, whose literal presence then becomes optional. The Holocaust can be reduced to the Six Million in most public presentations, or enlarged (for the sake of multicultural inclusion) into the Eleven Million whenever

Jews think it expedient. Jews have successfully figured Jewish Holocaust survivors and Jewish Holocaust deaths into synecdoches for the results of "racism," one part standing for the rest, so that other victims become semantically superfluous and need not be exhibited. It is a politically valuable symbolic structure that no activist Jew would willingly endanger, and hordes of White Holocaust survivors in a didactic version of Dachau are thus unthinkable.

This flexible structure has important practical consequences. A student being indoctrinated into the truths of multiracialism can learn his anti-racist lessons while contemplating only the Six Million, which is the normal educational practice in most Holocaust museums. "Because of its Jewish specificity," Yad Vashem's Avner Shalev argues, "[the Holocaust] should serve as a model in the global fight against the dangers of racism, anti-Semitism, ethnic hatred and genocide." Jewish specificity is somehow equivalent to human universality, so through the symbolic magic of the Holocaust we can commemorate crimes against any given minority by commemorating German crimes against Jews. If a Euro-American wants to rid himself of "racism" and learn tolerance for Blacks, he need only study German atrocities against Jehovah's Chosen People, whose victims during the Holocaust serve, in the words of philosopher Paul Ricoeur, as "delegates to our memory of all the victims of history."

As the result of a process purportedly involving nothing extrinsic to the events of the Holocaust, nothing so vulgar as Jewish media power, Jewish Holocaust victims have come to signify all other racial victims from time immemorial down to the present. Spielberg therefore presents the Eleven Million while dispensing with all visible evidence of any victims other than Jewish victims, a prerogative that the Holocaust entitles him to exercise. Indeed he gains the best of both worlds: He explicitly states the Eleven Million, signaling multicultural inclusion, while eradicating all Gentile camp inmates from the screen. His wildly unhistorical version of Dachau is an exact duplication of the ideological structure of an anti-racist Holocaust museum: Jewish victims stand for all other victims.

Yet in fact—and here we enter into the strange complexity of the Eleven Million—Spielberg's multicultural deference to the five million others, Falsehood #3, is more historically inaccurate than his racial devotion to the Six Million Jews. For the Eleven Million are bogus, pure fantasy. If the five million others who form the Holocaust's Gentile Auxiliary include all Allied civilians who died during the course of the war, the figure is far too low; if it means (as Spielberg intends) targeted ethnic minorities who perished in German concentration camps, it is far too high.[1]

Although revisionists seek to reduce the Six Million to some smaller number, it remains a genuine result of mainstream scholarship, whether it is true or not. No revisionist, furthermore, denies that millions of Jews were killed by Germans or died in German concentration camps.

The five million, on the other hand, are completely fictional and no Holocaust scholarship could ever account for their official recognition as co-victims with the Six. They were conjured up, on the basis of political expediency alone, by nazi-hunter Simon Wiesenthal in order to provide an emotional reason for non-Jews to commemorate the Holocaust, while retaining preeminent Jewish victimhood. Five million dead Gentiles are simply one million victims fewer than Six Million dead Jews, and that elementary arithmetic is literally the source of the Eleven Million victims that the Holocaust is officially supposed to com-

---

[1] See Peter Novick, *The Holocaust in American Life* (Boston: Houghton Mifflin, 1999), 215–16.

memorate, an obligation honored more in the breach than the observance. So by paying occasional lip service to the five million, Jews are falsifying history; by regularly ignoring them, they are unintentionally respecting the historical record.

Since most Americans have probably never heard of the five million, who constitute only a small part of the Holocaust's public mythology, we should not exaggerate their political significance. It is, however, worth noting the symbolic instability of this five million. Insofar as the five million are Gentiles they are *us*, our stake in the Jewish Holocaust, invented as a motive for our commemoration; insofar as they are "ethnic minorities" they are Other, not *us*, essentially surrogates for rainbow-coalition minorities, who can thereby be transported back into wartime history to teach anti-racist lessons. In the five million we are supposed not only to see ourselves but also to see the potential victims of our "racism," our reason for avoiding nazi-like racial self-assertion. A nonracialized interpretation of the five million would be useless for Holocaust lessons in racial tolerance; a five million comprised of powerless "ethnic minorities" provides an appropriate supplement to Judeocentric anti-racism.

Tens of millions of European deaths occurred in World War II, together with an incalculable number of casualties. Through Holocaust arithmetic they have all dwindled into one million less than Six Million, reduced to a symbolically ambiguous cohort of token Gentiles that Jews rarely even deign to exploit.

http://library.flawlesslogic.com/band.htm

THE MUFTI &
MARTIN HOHMANN

The length of an encyclopedia article indicates roughly the significance that the editors of the encyclopedia attach to the article's subject. In every encyclopedia Britain therefore receives more space than Bahrain. If you had never heard of either, you could accurately determine that the former is considered much more important than the latter simply by counting pages.

The same practical rule holds true in Holocaust Studies, though in a convoluted form.

The four-volume *Encyclopedia of the Holocaust* is a standard work in Holocaust Studies, consulted and cited by most scholars working in this rapidly expanding field. It displays an unmistakable fascination with the Grand Mufti of Jerusalem, who receives more attention within its pages than Goebbels, Goering, Eichmann, Heydrich, and even Himmler; the article on the Mufti is over twice as long as the article on Goebbels. Among the major personalities of NS Germany, only Adolf Hitler surpasses (just barely) the Mufti.

If you knew little about World War II, you could be forgiven for concluding that the Mufti was a towering figure in wartime German politics, never far from Hitler's side as they jointly plotted the innumerable nefarious schemes commonly attributed to nazi Germany: the burning of all non-Aryan books, the subjugation of the globe, the industrialized extermination of every Jew from Alaska to Zaire, and so forth.

There could be no more succinct example of how academic scholarship can be shaped to serve a contemporary political agenda. The *Encyclopedia of the Holocaust* devotes so many pages to the Mufti not because its editors and contributors want to illuminate the life of an intriguing figure in Mideast history, nor even because they want to attack belatedly an old enemy from sixty years ago. The Grand Mufti of Jerusalem receives a prominent role as a major perpetrator of the Jewish Holocaust because, in our time, Palestinian Arabs are enemies of the Jews, and the Mufti, the Palestinian religious leader Amin al-Husseini, conveniently supported Hitler.

The Mufti had escaped arrest by the British in mandatory Palestine and later arrived in Berlin seeking an alliance with the Germans, reasoning that his enemy's enemy should be his friend. He was a minor figure, at best, in NS Germany, but he has become a major figure for Jews today, his wartime activities regularly cited to suggest the ongoing nazi sympathies of modern Palestinians, and there are even fanciful tales of his gloating tours of extermination camps, where he would urge the nazis to run their gas chambers more efficiently. All of this is transparently political. If Hindus were fighting Jews today, Subhas Chandra Bose, the Indian nationalist leader who also arrived in Berlin seeking an alliance against a common enemy, would have been cast in the same sinister role that Amin al-Husseini now plays.

Jews have a powerful weapon, their Holocaust, and they want to deploy it against a current enemy, Palestinian Arabs. Jewish Holocaust scholarship has therefore been shaped to meet a specific political objective, contorting itself to make the Mufti into an important actor in the nazi state, thereby tainting Palestinian national aspirations and Palestinian resistance to Israeli occupation. Holocaust scholars hope to transform modern Palestinians into nazis, co-conspirators in the Jewish Holocaust, sharers in German guilt, and in terms of their political intentions Amin al-Husseini does genuinely become more significant than

Eichmann and Himmler. Holocaust Studies are racially aggressive Jewish politics conducted by scholarly means: The Palestinians are now an important enemy, more so than ever before, and Holocaust scholarship has been shaped accordingly.

Which brings us to Martin Hohmann, who evidently suffers from an incomplete understanding of the political character of the Holocaust.

Hohmann is the conservative German parliamentarian who aroused Jewish rage by alluding to massive Jewish participation in Marxist crimes in the former Soviet Union, and above all by drawing a dangerous conclusion: "Jews were in large numbers at the [Bolshevik] leadership level, as well as in Cheka execution squads. So one could with some justification describe Jews as a nation of perpetrators. That may sound frightening. But it would follow the same logic by which one describes Germans as a nation of perpetrators."

If a merciful God presided over political debates, Hohmann's poorly phrased argument would have worked, since it assumed a semitically-correct premise, the greatest of them all, the master premise that governs the rest: Thou shalt not blame Jews. More formally, any chain of reasoning that leads to an anti-Semitic conclusion must be false, because all such conclusions have been preemptively declared illegitimate, ruled wrong ahead of time. That's an unassailable, bedrock truth, acknowledged by all properly domesticated Gentiles, and on that solid foundation Hohmann built his argument.

It would be wrong to blame Jews today for the amply documented Marxist crimes that their forefathers committed decades ago in Russia, and throughout much of Europe it would be a frightening criminal offense to do so; therefore, Hohmann reasoned, it should also be wrong to blame Germans today for crimes of the nazi era. If Germans today are guilty of crimes in Germany's past, then Jews today must likewise be guilty of crimes in their Soviet past, a conclusion which would amount to prohibited anti-Semitism, blaming Jews as a group for Judeo-Bolshevik mass murder.

Hohmann, an opponent of the Berlin Holocaust memorial, was in fact saying, contrary to some press reports, that neither living Germans nor living Jews should be held guilty for crimes that dead Germans and dead Jews committed long ago. Neither Germans nor Jews should be viewed as a perpetrator people. His reasoning, though badly structured, was irrefutable, given its obligatory initial premise and its naive assumption of equality between Jews and Germans.

But of course Hohmann's argument did not work, and it has provoked outrage from Jews and even calls for a criminal investigation, chiefly because he attempted to use a semitically-correct premise for an impermissible purpose, exculpating living Germans. He does not want the Jewish Holocaust to remain forever a central part of German identity, and he knows that no healthy nation would elevate a crime into the defining event of its history. He thought he had discovered a safe logical device, operating at the edges of the rules that control discussions of the Holocaust, proving that Germans should not permanently identify themselves as the world's foremost perpetrator nation. He was obviously wrong.

Although revisionists question many of the events the fall under the rubric "Holocaust," Hohmann was doing nothing of the sort. Yet his argument was, despite his apparent naivety, just as dangerous as revisionism, perhaps more so, since it challenged the Jewish Holocaust at the level of its political objectives, of which historical facts are (as we have seen) merely the malleable vehicle, subject to creative alteration whenever the need arises.

Jews in Germany saw Hohmann's argument for what it was: not merely an irritating allusion to old Jewish crimes, but also an attack on the power of their Holocaust weapon. A Holocaust weapon that no longer inflicted perpetual German penance would be unholocaustal, deprived of one of its desired effects. Jews want Germans to feel weak and guilty; that's what Holocaust commemoration in Germany is really about.

So Paul Spiegel, president of Germany's Central Council of Jews, quickly convinced himself that Hohmann's semitically-correct argument amounted to "a reach into the lowest drawer of disgusting anti-Semitism." Such angry denunciations, and there were many, have a number of practical goals, but the most important is surely the warning that they give to others: You can't talk this way, and if you do, we'll work hard to punish you.

The Holocaust is a contrived instrument of Jewish power, and if it ceased to be an effective weapon that Jews can wield against their enemies whenever they choose, it wouldn't, from their perspective, be worth the trouble of writing all those Holocaust books and erecting all those Holocaust temples that commemorate it. The main purpose of the Jewish Holocaust is to attack enemies of the Jews in the present, and since Jews in the present still hate Germans, they will vilify and punish any German who attempts to disarm their favorite weapon, even a polite German who dutifully obeys their rules.

National Vanguard, November 5, 2003

THE HOLOCAUST AS WEAPON

Rabbi Dov Fischer, vice-president of the Zionist Organization of America, is very angry. He knows that Europeans are less supportive of Israel than Americans, and he feels himself filling with righteous fury at their presumption. It is time, he has decided, to deploy the Jewish Holocaust:

> We [Jews] remember that the food they eat is grown from soil fertilized by 2,000 years of Jewish blood they have sprinkled onto it. Atavistic Jew-hatred lingers in the air into which the ashes rose from the crematoria. Finally, the best of Europe truly are wracked by the burdened conscience of what they, their parents and their *bubbes* and *zeides* did, or failed to do, in the 1940s. So, instead of confronting a shameful past that belies their self-vaunted Romantic civilization, they seek now to assuage their consciences with the mendacity that Israel 2002 is no different from Europe 1942.[1]

Rabbi Fischer's metaphors are not fully consistent. He doesn't really mean that the food White Europeans eat required the shedding of Jewish blood; he means that Europeans have been permanently tainted by their long history of violent anti-Semitism, which has become an essential part of the European character, just as the food we eat

---

[1] Dov Fischer, "We're Right, the Whole World's Wrong," http://www.forward.com/issues/2002/02.04.19/oped3.html (April 19, 2002).

becomes part of our bodies. The Jewish Holocaust, in Rabbi Fischer's opinion, was the most notable expression of the "atavistic Jew-hatred" that has always pervaded Europe, forming part of the oxygen that Europeans breathe, which they now inhale along with the ashes still circulating from the nazi crematoria. In other words, all Europeans form a single perpetrator people.

An American or a British war veteran fifty years ago would not have recognized Rabbi Fischer's vision of European history. For them, there was only one major perpetrator people in Europe (Germans), along with several lesser perpetrator peoples (Italians, Croats, etc.). Their war had liberated the subject nations of Europe from fascist tyranny, which presupposed that the nations tyrannized by the Axis merited liberating. They were good people yearning to be free, and the Allies nobly freed them at great sacrifice. The old view of the war may have been a simplification and it may even have been an outright falsehood, but whatever its deficiencies it was not anti-European and it assumed the essential goodness of the West.

Most Americans and Britons probably still accept some form of the heroic interpretation of World War II, wherein the Allied victory in Europe brought an end to a dark barbarism that threatened Western civilization; very few Jews do, and their Holocaust is an ideological tool designed for the purpose, among others, of dismantling it. Rabbi Fischer's is the authentic voice of the Jewish Holocaust. He angrily directs his Holocaust weapon not only against Germans but against all Europeans, regardless of the side their nations fought on during Europe's Civil War. (The Jewish neo-conservative Charles Krauthammer has repeated Fischer's charges in less flamboyant language. Both have been angered by anti-Israel sentiments in Europe.)

It is no doubt politically useful for Jews in Germany to retain the old mythology of unique German evil, and they will fight hard against any German patriot who challenges it. Their special status in Germany requires special German guilt for crimes against Jews, which is best preserved by permanent institutions like the coming Holocaust memorial in Berlin. But unique German evil is far less useful for Jews everywhere else, for the obvious reason that it exculpates everyone who isn't a German. In the US the Holocaust has therefore become a special American responsibility, and no Holocaust museum would be complete without some tendentious account of culpable American failure to prevent it. Americans, a spokeswoman for the Washington Holocaust Museum once alleged, were "just as guilty" as the Germans. Wherever the Holocaust travels, its promoters will discover deep, nazi-like guilt in any population foolish enough to commemorate it, and that unfortunately includes most Western nations.

One of the strengths of the Holocaust is the set of informal and formal rules that discourages anyone from mentioning the racial motivations that underlie it. In *Hitler's Willing Executioners*, Daniel Goldhagen discovered a unique "eliminationist anti-Semitism" in the German people. In his more recent study of Catholic responsibility for the Holocaust (*A Moral Reckoning*) he discovered the same "eliminationist anti-Semitism" at the heart of the Catholic Church, which was "centrally animated" by Jew-hatred and has not yet properly atoned for its "demonology of Jews." When Goldhagen turned his gaze upon the Serbs, legitimate heroes in the old version of the war, he found an "eliminationist politics" and a "virulent variant of the nationalism characteristic of Western civilization." Clearly, Goldhagen's initial claim that Germans are uniquely guilty, in an almost genetic sense, has been contradicted by his subsequent findings. We are dealing here with *ad hoc* denunciations concealed under the guise of serious scholarship. Goldhagen will discover the same pathology wherever he looks in Europe. That's because he is a racially committed Jew attacking his enemy, and his enemy happens to be all of us. He thus freely distributes nazi evil, despite his earlier belief that it was a malign property specific to the German people.

Another strength of the Holocaust is its doctrine of uniqueness. If you sign on with the Holocaust, you are expected to accept its crucial non-comparison clause, which is clearly stated in Holocaust scholarship. According to the authoritative *Encyclopedia of the Holocaust*, comparing the Holocaust to other crimes is a form of "Holocaust denial." For historian Deborah Lipstadt, denial of Holocaust uniqueness is "far more insidious than outright denial." Elie Wiesel goes further: Any attempt to "demystify" or "desanctify" the Holocaust is anti-Semitic. For Holocaust historians and popularizers, their subject matter is an ahistorical event, incomparable to and apart from all other events. Even Raul Hilberg, one of the more moderate Holocaustologists, has called the Holocaust "the defining moment in the drama of good and evil." The Holocaust does not merely demand belief in a collection of events; it demands belief in their immeasurable world-historical significance.

Martin Hohmann now denies that he ever intended to question the "uniqueness" of the Holocaust. In a literal sense this concession is meaningless, since all historical events are equally unique, just as an ant is as unique as an elephant. Whatever the Holocaust includes in its often dubious historical claims, it can be no more unique than any other event, even if every word of the official story is true. Yet in a more important sense Hohmann was indeed guilty of diminishing Holocaust uniqueness. In the special language of the Holocaust "uniqueness" means in practice "of infinitely greater magnitude." Jewish suffering during World War II was far greater and far more significant than any other suffering in history, so much greater and so much more significant that the Holocaust stands categorically apart from all other crimes, and that's why it is so imperative that every Western capital should be endowed with some permanent memorial commemorating it. There can be nothing similar to the Jewish Holocaust, and by implicitly comparing the Holocaust to Judeo-Bolshevik mass murder, as though they were events of the same kind, Hohmann was diminishing Holocaust uniqueness, in the special meaning of "uniqueness" that the Holocaust arrogates to itself.

In academic accounts of the Ukrainian Ethnocide, the Ukrainian death-toll ranges from three million (Robert Conquest) to as high as seven million (i.e. one million more than six); a common figure is just over five million. Conquest calls this the only entirely man-made famine in history, so Ukrainians could, if they wanted to imitate the belligerent Jewish model of vocal victimhood, call their holocaust completely unique, incomparable to and categorically apart from all other events. They could also attempt to promote their holocaust as a permanent source of shame for all Western nations that failed to prevent it. But they wouldn't succeed, because even if they felt the same anti-Western hostility that motivates activist Jews like Goldhagen, Ukrainians do not have the political power to enforce their vision of history on everyone else.

No reasonable person could deny that the Ukrainian Ethnocide is at least comparable in its severity to the Jewish Holocaust. On its face the Holocaust's claim of categorical uniqueness is false, and we need no revisionist arguments to see that. Hence the rules of Holocaust correctness, invoked by Michel Friedman, which have been contrived to protect the Holocaust from all competing holocausts: The Jewish Holocaust is so radically unique that any comparison of it to other events amounts to anti-Semitism and relativizing Holocaust denial. Those rules are now an intrinsic part of the Holocaust, embedded in its scholarship and routinely invoked by its advocates, and though few Jews would openly admit it, the rules clearly imply the belief that Jewish deaths are much more significant than other deaths. Insofar as we accept "relativizing" the Holocaust as a thought-crime, as apparently almost everyone in official Germany does, we are in effect submitting to a view of history that privileges Jewish lives over non-Jewish lives. It makes perfect sense for the Jewish state of Israel to commemorate this Judeocentrism; it is very foolish for anyone else to follow their example.

Jews have, to borrow Wiesel's language, successfully mystified and sanctified their Holocaust, removing it from history and fashioning it into a racial weapon that they can wield freely against their enemies, confident (because of the rules prohibiting anti-Semitism) that their enemies will not reply in kind. To recognize that the Holocaust is an instrument of Jewish power, we need only observe how it is deployed; to recognize that it is a contrived instrument, we need only analyze how the racially self-interested ideas embedded in it, like the doctrine of categorical uniqueness, serve to protect and enhance its effectiveness.

National Vanguard (online), November 11, 2003

THE PATRIOT:
REVIEWING A REVIEW

Excerpts from Jewish film critic Jonathan Foreman's "The Nazis, er, the Redcoats are coming!," a review of *The Patriot:*

The Patriot presents a deeply sentimental cult of the family, casts unusually Aryan-looking heroes. . . .

If the Nazis had won the war in Europe, and their propaganda ministry had decided to make a film about the American Revolution, *The Patriot* is exactly the movie you could expect to see. . . .

In one scene towheaded preteens are armed by their father and turned into the equivalent of the Werwolf boy-soldiers that the Third Reich was thought to have recruited from the Hitler Youth to carry out guerrilla attacks against the invading Allies.

In the film's most exciting sequence, [Mel] Gibson is provoked by the foreigner into becoming one of those bloodied, ax-wielding forest supermen so beloved in Nazi folk-iconography: an 18th-century equivalent of the Goth leader Arminius (aka Hermann the German) who annihilated two Roman Legions in the Teutoburger Forest.

The most outrageous of *The Patriot*'s many faults is the way [director Roland] Emmerich and [screenwriter Robert] Rodat show the British troops committing a war crime that closely resembles one of the most notorious Nazi war crimes of World War II — the massacre of 642 people (including 205 children) in the French village of Oradour sur Glane on June 10, 1944. The film mimics the horrible event with clear accuracy and turns it into just another atrocity committed by redcoats in 1780.... At Oradour, the Waffen SS "Das Reich" division punished local resistance activity by first shooting all the men and boys. Then they rounded up the women and children, locked them in the town church and set it afire.

[*The Patriot* casts] George III's redcoats as cartoonish paragons of evil who commit one monstrous—but wholly invented—atrocity after another.... If you didn't know anything about the Revolution, you might actually believe the British army in North America was made up of astonishingly cruel, even demonic, sadists who really did do this kind of thing—as if they were the 18th century equivalent of the Nazi SS.

You could actually argue without too much exaggeration that *The Patriot* is as fascist a film (and I use the term in its literal sense, not as a synonym for "bad") as anything made in decades.

Emmerich and Rodat—unwittingly or not—have done something unpleasantly akin to Holocaust revisionism. They have made a film that will have the effect of inoculating audiences against the unique historical horror of Oradour—and implicitly rehabilitating the Nazis while making the British seem as evil as history's worst monsters.[1]

For anyone interested in the insidious character of "antinazi" propaganda—with which, of course, we're still bombarded almost daily, more than a half century after NS Germany's defeat—Jonathan Foreman's review of *The Patriot* is worth examining.

I happen to agree with its general argument: *The Patriot*

---

[1] http://www.salon.com/2000/07/03/patriot_3/

presents a grossly inaccurate depiction of British soldiers during the American Revolution, casting the British as cartoonishly evil villains while fabricating horrific crimes, repeated acts of what Foreman calls "bestial cruelty," that they never committed.

Foreman's review focuses on two contrasting historical facts, in themselves perhaps undeniable: During the Revolutionary War British soldiers did not burn down a church with American civilians inside, an episode that nevertheless appears in Roland Emmerich's film, but in 1944, at Oradour-sur-Glane, German SS soldiers did burn down a church with French civilians inside. *The Patriot* thus falsely presents British soldiers as though they were like "nazis" — that is, "demonic sadists" guilty of unparalleled, gratuitous violence against noncombatants.

Now there is some question whether SS soldiers actually did set fire to the church at Oradour, and good evidence that at least a few risked their lives attempting to save French civilians trapped inside. But let's stipulate that the story is essentially true and that the "nazi" war crime in question occurred more or less as advertised.

What is absent from Foreman's Oradour reference, like all the now ubiquitous contemporary references in the popular media to "nazi" atrocities, is any *before*, any set of antecedent events that might explain why German soldiers would burn down a church filled with French women and children. We are left instead only with the "bestial cruelty" of "nazi" war criminals—demonic, sadistic, unprovoked, incomprehensible by normal standards of historical explanation.

Foreman tells us, correctly, that it is wrong to present British soldiers in the Revolutionary War as "cartoonish paragons of evil," but he believes, and he assumes that his audience will also believe, that there is one authentic set of "paragons of evil" whose sadistic violence isn't at all cartoonish. Only "nazis" are really capable of the "bestial cruelty" *The Patriot* falsely attributes to the British. That, briefly, is Foreman's principal explicit complaint; I will get to his more implicit concerns in a moment.

But were German soldiers, even German Waffen-SS soldiers, themselves really like "nazis"? In other words, did "nazis" — demonic Germans who killed gratuitously, gleefully, more savagely than any other set of killers in history — even exist during World War II? Or were German soldiers simply like any other soldiers, capable of criminal retaliation against civilians when provoked, but no different in kind from any other occupying army facing determined resistance from a hostile population?

Here are some facts about the events that preceded Oradour,[2] the *before* that allusions to "nazi" war crimes regularly ignore, represented in this case only by the "local resistance activity" (an apparently innocuous *before*) that Foreman briefly mentions:

❖ On June 9, 1944, the day before the Oradour massacre, the SS division *Das Reich* recapture the town of Tulle, which had fallen into the hands of French partisans. There they find the mutilated corpses of sixty-two German soldiers who, after surrendering to the Resistance, had been butchered: "Some had had their genitals cut off and stuffed into their mouths. Others had been covered with excrement. One man had holes in his heels with a rope through them, and a [smashed]

---

[2] The quotations that appear in the following summary of events are from H. W. Koch, "Background to Oradour," *Aspects of the Third Reich*, ed. H. W. Koch (New York: St. Martin's Press, 1985), 386–89, and Marc Rikmenspoel's "Tulle and Oradour: The German View," http://www.oradour.info/appendix/rikmen01.htm.

face, indicating that he had been tied to the back of a truck and driven around."

❖ Also on June 9, the Germans learn that French partisans have captured SS-Sturmbannführer Helmut Kämpfe, a popular officer, and plan to publicly burn him alive in Oradour, a center of partisan activity.

❖ On June 10, in an attempt to rescue Kämpfe, a company of the SS regiment *Der Führer*, under the command of Stubaf. Adolf Dickmann, enters Oradour and discovers "a smoldering German army ambulance in which the driver and co-driver had been chained to the steering wheel and burnt alive together with their wounded passengers."

❖ Dickmann takes hostages and houses the women and children in the local church. The Germans hope to exchange the male hostages for Kämpfe, Dickmann's close personal friend.

❖ The Germans search the town for arms, discovering caches of illicit weapons in almost all the houses. (Partisan warfare, it should be remembered, is not sanctioned by international conventions and is technically illegal.)

❖ The Germans discover another smoldering body, which they identify as Kämpfe. The partisans have, as the Germans feared, burned him alive.

❖ Dickmann then, according to the conventional account of the Oradour massacre, orders the male hostages shot and orders his men to set fire to the church, incinerating all but three of the women and children inside.

❖ The SS institutes court-martial proceedings against Dickmann, a clear indication that Oradour-like war crimes were not routine SS behavior. Dickmann will later die in Normandy without coming to trial.

Now the *before*, the antecedent events that explain the war crime, Foreman's "local resistance activity," does not excuse Oradour. It does, however, eliminate from it the crucial element that makes "nazi" war-crime allusions so rhetorically powerful—the implied charge of sadistic, gratuitous cruelty. We now know that savagery preceded Oradour, to which SS savagery was a response.

We also know that any group of soldiers, including American or British soldiers, might very well have retaliated in a similar way under similar circumstances. German soldiers, even German SS soldiers fighting the celebrated Resistance in France, are thus revealed as normal men, no different from ourselves. They cease to be "demonic sadists" and "history's worst monsters."

If aging SS veterans commissioned a film in which the atrocities committed against Germans at and around Oradour figured prominently, but no reference to German retaliation were made, we would call the film dishonestly misleading. Not literally false, because the French atrocities did in fact occur, but a serious deception nevertheless, because our hypothetical SS film would leave the impression that only French partisans committed war crimes. The same is true of the Oradour reference as it is exploited in Foreman's review and as it regularly appears in litanies of allegedly unique German savagery.

In almost any war one side can be dishonestly demonized even by a truthful enumeration of its crimes, if the crimes of its adversaries are suppressed. That just recently occurred in media accounts of Serb atrocities in Kosovo, and for illustrative purposes I practiced my own version of this deception by omission earlier. I neglected to mention that at Tulle, after the SS discovered the mutilated bodies of their comrades, they retaliated by hanging ninety-nine Frenchmen. That additional fact, an understandable but still criminal act of revenge, obviously changes our evaluation of the event; Germans become perpetrators of a war crime in addition to being innocent victims. Tulle can be turned into an example of typical French barbarism by suppressing, as I did, the *after*, and an example of typical German barbarism by suppressing the *before*. The latter in fact happened: Tulle now appears among the list of German atrocities in occupied France, another sadistic "nazi" war crime, because the sixty-two Germans tortured and murdered by the Resistance have been studiously omitted from popular accounts of the event.

The deceptive propaganda image of the "nazi" has, after more than five decades of such omissions, entered everyone's mental repertoire of familiar historical references, so whenever a writer wants to evoke uniquely evil "bestial cruelty," he simply summons up the "nazis" and everyone will know what he means. The propaganda image of the "nazi" also serves contemporary political objectives, which accounts for its longevity. The old Manichean mythology of the Second World War, which contrasts the Allies as the heroic forces of Good to the Axis as the embodiment of absolute Evil, is the legitimating narrative of the current anti-national, anti-racialist political order, and it requires unique "nazi" evil to sustain it.

About seventy years ago, so the story runs, a reign of unprecedented cruelty and violence was unleashed upon the world, a dark, atavistic assault on human civilization that the Allied forces of light heroically defeated, just barely. This evil still lurks beneath the surface of the Western civilization from which it erupted, even in the nations responsible for its defeat, and we all must therefore be vigilant that no similar eruptions occur again. The perpetual "diversity" campaigns in the Western democracies against "intolerance" and "hate" are necessary prophylactic measures, mandated by the enormity of the horror they are meant to prevent, against a recurrence of the absolute, metaphysical evil that the "nazis" briefly incarnated.

Accordingly, whatever characterized NS Germany — its "racism," to cite the most important example — is bad and its contrary good; you merely need to learn that Hitler supported 'X' to know that 'X' is wrong. That's why Jonathan Foreman is so insistent that "nazi" evil must be reserved for authentic "nazis," that no one but National Socialist Germans ("history's worst monsters") should be shown committing "nazi"-like crimes ("unique historical horror[s]"). Any hint that such crimes are a tragic but common part of most modern wars would undermine the near-universal belief in unique "nazi" evil and threaten the programmatic anti-racialism that the political Left has successfully erected upon it.

Not surprisingly, the subtext of Foreman's review, hardly even concealed, is White "racism." Hence his otherwise inconsequential description of the film's "unusually Aryan-looking heroes." He means, of course, that they look too White, too much like the bestial "nazis" who regularly committed unprecedented acts of sadistic violence during World War II. White physical features, absent a sufficiently multiracial cast, absent Morgan Freeman in an anachronistic supporting role, now conjure up, in the eyes of not a few liberals, the specter of mass murder.

Foreman could have selected the Soviet massacre of Ukrainians at Vinnytsia as his *locus classicus* for real "bestial cruelty." Or, had he wished to be bolder, he could have selected the American massacre of Vietnamese peasants at My Lai. Unpublishably bolder would have been the Jewish massacre of Palestianian civilians at Deir Yassin, which coincidentally offers a close parallel to another atrocity scene in *The Patriot*. But none of these comparable crimes would have suited his underlying political concerns, none would have resonated as effectively as "nazi" atrocities in a film review that faults director Emmerich—himself German, Foreman is careful to point out—for casting "unusually Aryan-looking [and thus sinister] heroes."

We can now understand why a liberal Jew would see "fascism" in a cinematic account of the American Revolution. Although he tells us that he "use[s] the term in its literal sense, not as a synonym for 'bad,'" "fascism" in its literal sense appears nowhere in Foreman's review. Its real synonyms are, clearly, White racialism and political nationalism. No sooner has he detached "nazi"-like crimes from the British Redcoats than Foreman assigns them instead to *The Patriot*'s American Rebels, who remind him of "Werwolf boy-soldiers" (themselves a fiction, incidentally) and the "bloodied, ax-wielding forest supermen so beloved in Nazi folk-iconography." Foreman, and in this respect he can stand in for most of the System's spokesmen, is frightened by seeing White Americans with guns (or even axes) fighting for American national liberty. He thinks he's really seeing "nazis."

Conflating Euro-American patriots with genocidal "nazis" is multiracialism's response to its growing sense of unease at American national history. Most nations, and all healthy nations, maintain some sense of historical continuity between their national beginnings and their present reality; a nation that loses respect for its past, and a well-founded belief that its present is a natural evolution from it, is fast losing its nationhood. Contemporary multicultural America, however, rests on the increasingly implausible lie that the Founding Fathers and the Patriots who shed their blood for political liberty would have approved of the shape our balkanizing multiracial empire has assumed, that they really envisioned the nation they fought to create resembling southern California, that they were all early exponents of multiracial "diversity" and the abolition of national borders. The White Patriots of 1776 are therefore now embarrassing to liberal multiracialists because they know, although most Euro-Americans have not yet caught on, that the founders of the American Republic would be shocked by multiracial morass into which it has descended, that the America of the present is so increasingly distant from its beginnings that it is rapidly becoming an entirely different country. On issues surrounding race Thomas Jefferson, some multiracialist liberals now (rightly) suspect, had far more in common with Adolf Hitler than with Bill Clinton.

Embarrassed liberal disquiet at the national past is not exclusive to the United States. The anti-nationalist establishment in Germany is embarrassed by old-fashioned patriotic reverence for Hermann the Cheruscan; its counterpart in France is embarrassed by old-fashioned patriotic reverence for Charles Martel and Joan of Arc. Old-fashioned European national heroes, unlike modern European politicians, disapproved of foreigners on their nation's soil and fought to expel them, a motive not dissimilar from the "xenophobia" that animated the rebels of 1776, who had come to regard the British as foreigners on their soil as well and, after an almost exclusively White revolution, successfully expelled them, winning national independence in the process.

At the outset I called "anti-nazi" propaganda "insidious" because, unlike false statements of fact, which can easily be refuted, it relies instead on false or skewed presuppositions—supposed "facts," forming part of everyone's common knowledge, that lie behind explicit statements while carrying their own unexamined political meanings. The "fact" that "nazis" were guilty of unprecedented, demonically sadistic war crimes says nothing explicit about White Americans or White Australians or White Swedes etc., but it carries the unexamined and uncontested political meaning that racial feelings among each are similarly evil and can easily erupt into similar horrors. Those are "truths" that everyone "knows" and no one need demonstrate.

Jonathan Foreman's review is thus revealing for expressing, more clearly than most multiracialist media commentary, how the myth of unique "nazi" evil has been broadened to embrace all expressions of White national patriotism.

http://library.flawlesslogic.com/patriot.htm

GIBSON, JESUS, & THE JEWS

GIBSON CAPITULATES

Mel Gibson is passionately angry at critics of his upcoming film about the death of Jesus Christ.

In remarks quoted in the *New Yorker* magazine, he denied "The Passion" is anti-Semitic and accused some of those leading the chorus against the film of being "anti-Christian." Gibson said he personally has been the target of "vehement anti-Christian sentiment."

[...]

As proof of his desire to avoid confrontation, Gibson cited his decision to cut a scene in which Caiaphas says "his blood be on us and on our children" soon after Pontius Pilate washes his hands of the captive Christ.

"I wanted it in," he said. "My brother said I was wimping out if I didn't include it. But, man, if I included that in there, they'd be coming after me at my house. They'd come to kill me."[1]

The WorldNetDaily story excerpted above is entitled "A passionate Mel Gibson strikes back against critics," but it actually details Gibson's reluctant capitulation to Jewish power. The script of *The Passion*, his upcoming film about Christ's Crucifixion, was initially intended to be a scrupulously faithful adaptation of the gospels; it has now been revised in an attempt to silence vociferous Jewish objec-

---

[1] http://www.wnd.com/news/article.asp?ARTICLE_ID=34497

tions. Gibson is, as his brother suspected, "wimping out," putting his fear of Jewish anger above his professed religious beliefs.

The scene that Gibson cut itself represented a concession to Jewish sensitivities. According to the New Testament, "his blood be upon us and upon our children" was shouted by a Jewish mob ("the whole people" in the Catholic Douay-Rheims translation), not simply by Caiaphas, a high priest in the Jerusalem Temple (Matthew 27.25; cf. 1 Thessalonians 2.14–16). That major concession—removing the verse from a Jewish mob and assigning it to a single Jewish priest—was nevertheless unacceptable to organized Jewry, so Gibson has now excised the entire scene, fearing Jewish retaliation. "Fear of the Jews" (*ton phobon tôn Ioudaiôn*) is, incidentally, a New Testament phrase (e.g. John 7.13).

Conservative Christians believe that all sacred scripture is inspired by God (2 Timothy 3.16). The operative theological term is *theopneustos* in the Greek New Testament, *divinitus inspirata* in the Latin Vulgate, the preferred translation for traditionalist Catholics like Gibson. Sacred scripture is of divine origin, a longstanding Christian belief that was proclaimed as irrevocable dogma at the Council of Trent, the Church council that forms the basis for Gibson's brand of Catholicism.

In simpler terms, the events reported in the New Testament are present in the text because God wants them to be there. Not all details pertaining to Christ's Crucifixion are recorded in the various New Testament accounts, but those that were recorded express almighty God's intentions. They are historical facts that God wants mankind to know, which is why he inspired the four evangelists to write them down. If God were the director of Gibson's film, "his blood be upon us and upon our children" would appear in the script, just as it appears in the New Testament.

The orchestrated Jewish campaign against *The Passion* left Gibson with a choice between placating Jews and accurately dramatizing what he regards as the inspired Word of God, and he chose the former. To his credit, he stood up to Jewish pressure longer than most Christians would have, but the final result is the same as if he had capitulated on the first day. Jewish organizations have successfully asserted their right to oversee Christian depictions of the central event of the Christian religion. No film of Christ's death can be shown in American theaters without a Jewish imprimatur. The New Testament is anti-Semitic hate-speech.

For those of us who are not Christians, Gibson's capitulation confirms our suspicion of modern Christianity's weakness, despite its numerical strength in the United States. It would be impossible to envisage the fathers of the Catholic Church or the heroes of the Protestant Reformation acknowledging, as Gibson has, the right of anti-Christian Jews to act as censors of Christian sacred scripture. If you believe, as Gibson does, that the Christian God inspired the New Testament, you shouldn't listen to the exegetical opinions of Abraham Foxman, who (after all) doesn't believe in the Christian God and doesn't accept his New Testament. Pious Jews believe, on the contrary, that Jesus suffers five deaths a day in Hell, one in boiling excrement.

We should also note an historical irony. Jews oppose any faithful dramatization of the Christian account of Christ's death because it would suggest Jewish responsibility for deicide. As the ADL's Foxman complained, "the [unrevised] film unambiguously portrays Jewish authorities and the Jewish mob as the ones responsible for the decision to crucify Jesus." Yet on this subject the Christian New Testament and the Jewish Talmud are in complete agreement, a fact which the Jewish organizations attacking

Gibson would never freely admit:

> According to the Talmud, Jesus was executed by a proper rabbinical court for idolatry, inciting other Jews to idolatry, and contempt of rabbinical authority. All classical Jewish sources which mention his execution are quite happy to take responsibility for it; in the talmudic account the Romans are not even mentioned.
>
> The more popular accounts—which were nevertheless taken quite seriously—such as the notorious *Toldot Yeshu* are even worse, for in addition to the above crimes they accuse him of witchcraft. The very name "Jesus" was for Jews a symbol of all that is abominable, and this popular tradition still persists.[2]

In other words, a faithful Talmudic version of Christ's Crucifixion would not, on the contentious issue of Jewish responsibility, be any different from the film that Mel Gibson planned to make, before "fear of the Jews" convinced him to revise God's inspired script.

http://library.flawlesslogic.com/passion.htm

---

[2] Israel Shahak, *Jewish History, Jewish Religion: The Weight of Three Thousand Years* (London: Pluto Press, 1994), 97–98.

JESUS & THE ADL

Are Jews *today* responsible for the Crucifixion of Jesus two thousand years ago? An ABC News poll indicated that fewer than one in ten Americans believe that they are. Were Jews *two thousand years ago* responsible for the Crucifixion of Jesus? A recent poll by the Jewish Anti-Defamation League (ADL) indicates that one in four Americans believe that they were. "It is troubling," says Abraham Foxman, the ADL's National Director, "that so many Americans already accept the notion of Jewish guilt. We are concerned that Mr. Gibson's film—with its unambiguous blaming of the Jews—will not only reinforce those views, but could exacerbate the problem by convincing even more people that his version of the story of the Crucifixion is Gospel truth."

The two questions are, of course, significantly different. Belief in Jewish guilt today for an event two thousand years ago is irrational, assuming a magical transmission of acquired collective culpability over many generations. On the other hand, belief in historical Jewish complicity in the Crucifixion is tantamount to belief in the accuracy of the New Testament, where crucial Jewish involvement in the Messiah's death is amply documented.

"He came unto his own," the evangelist John wrote, "and his own received him not" (John 1.11). The nascent Christian Church, though comprised largely of Jews, believed that their anti-Christian compatriots had engineered Christ's execution, and Christian writers recorded that belief for posterity. See especially 1 Thessalonians 2.14-16, which belongs to one of the earliest Christian texts, written independently of the gospel passion stories. In the gospels themselves Jewish leaders work for Jesus' death, the Sanhedrin decides his fate, the Roman prefect Pontius Pilate reluctantly complies, a Jewish mob accepts guilt for the imminent deicide (Matthew 27.25), and Roman soldiers torment the Christian Son of God before crucifying him.

That sequence of events has been central to Christianity for two millennia. It is corroborated in large measure by the Jewish historian Josephus (*Antiquities of the Jews* 18.3) and even by the Talmud, and it provides the basic plot for Mel Gibson's *Passion of the Christ*, the film which prompted both opinion polls. Gibson could honestly answer "no" to the first question, and he has done so regularly. But he has been reluctant to deny the historicity of the New Testament, and he has drawn angry criticism as a result. "The Jews' real complaint," as he has correctly pointed out, "isn't with my film but with the gospels."

The second question—the ADL's question—could be rephrased: Do you believe the New Testament account of the Crucifixion? That was what the ADL were really asking. They were disappointed with the meager results from the previous ABC poll, and their own question was clearly designed to increase the number of respondents who would give the "wrong" answer, thus falling into the category "anti-Semite." Thirty-nine percent of Americans define themselves as born-again Christians, most of them committed to the Bible's literal inerrancy, so the only real surprise from the ADL poll is the unexpectedly low number who unwittingly characterized themselves as anti-Semitic. If you've read the New Testament and if you believe that its account of Christ's final days is more or less true, then (according to the ADL) you represent a troubling social problem. You have joined the ranks of irrational anti-Semites. Your religious beliefs require restructuring, and your scriptures must be drastically rewritten to prevent others from succumbing to your error.

Jesus & the ADL

The ADL were familiar with the ABC poll, which they refer to in their press release.[1] They asked a much different question in order to generate artificially a larger number of Christian anti-Semites. Conservative Christians should ask themselves why a major Jewish organization would define anti-Semitism so broadly that anyone who believes in the historical accuracy of the gospels would fail their test. Why would the ADL define belief in the New Testament, which most Christians consider a divinely inspired document, as troubling evidence of anti-Semitism?

Part of the answer lies in the character of minority politics. For all minority activists the best kind of racial hatred is a racial hatred you can falsely prove without having to experience the painful consequences that would occur if the hatred were genuine. For partisans of Black political causes the dragging death of James Byrd was the best evidence of alleged White racial hatred because it was so unrepresentative; most interracial crime is Black-on-White. From the propaganda onslaught surrounding Byrd's death Black political activists acquired false proof of widespread White "racism" without having to endure the effects of actual racial hatred. If Byrd's killers were indeed representative of a substantial proportion of Euro-Americans, life for Blacks would quickly become unpleasant. Since most Whites are non-racialist, proving White "racism" by such a wildly atypical interracial crime conferred on Blacks the political benefits of vicarious victimhood, free from even the threat of any real victimization.

The ADL poll reflects a similar strategy and relies on a similar passivity in the people they are attempting to malign. The charge of anti-Semitism is potentially so devas-

---

[1] http://www.adl.org/PresRele/ASUS_12/4454_12.htm

tating today precisely because the number of Whites who oppose Jewish power is, unfortunately, so low. The certainty that anti-Semitism is not only scarce but also widely reviled motivates Jewish attempts to manufacture bogus evidence of it and to expand the range of beliefs the label includes. We would find such calculated deception degrading; Jewish organizations think it's simply clever politics.

It is perfectly possible for a Christian to believe that Jews killed Jesus two thousand years ago and still have nothing but warm feelings for Jews today. Christians who accept the Bible's historical inerrancy are, as a matter of undoubted fact, the strongest supporters of Jews. Most are ardent Zionists, and most believe, wrongly but sincerely, that Christianity identifies Jews as God's Chosen People (cf. Galatians 3.28–29). The ADL have consciously defined their most devoted admirers as though they were their worst enemies, secure in the knowledge that few of them will object. Pat Robertson will not renounce his Likudnik Zionism and his servile philo-Semitism just because the ADL has in effect called him an anti-Semite.

Dr. Pierce once described the Jews as gamblers, never satisfied with success, always looking for risky new victories. The ADL's recent polling legerdemain is a minor case in point. A reasonable Jew would be content with the routine repudiations of collective Jewish guilt for Christ's death that now flow steadily from all mainstream Christian spokesmen, including Mel Gibson. But the Jewish gamblers at the ADL want much more: They want Christians to rewrite the New Testament, and they want them to feel guilty that they ever believed it in the first place.

http://library.flawlesslogic.com/passion_02.htm

Jewish Hypocrisy & the One-State Solution

Abraham Foxman, national director of the Anti-Defamation League (ADL), America's leading anti-White organization, is once again suffering from one of his recurrent bouts of sanctimonious outrage. The cause of his most recent outrage is Michael Tarazi's proposal for a "one-state solution" to the Arab-Israeli conflict, a proposal which Foxman says "exemplifies arrogance at its height."

Tarazi, a Harvard-educated legal adviser to the Palestine Liberation Organization, has suggested in a *New York Times* op-ed article that Palestinians, rather than working for a separate state of their own, as most Mideast diplomacy envisions, should instead pursue "a one-state solution in which citizens of all faiths and ethnicities live together as equals." Israeli Jews in turn should learn to "view Palestinian Christians and Muslims not as demographic threats but as fellow citizens." Tarazi's model for the de-Zionizing of Israel is multiracial democracy in South Africa, where Whites voluntarily surrendered their racial dominance to Blacks and now, according to fanciful reports in the controlled media, enjoy all the benefits that an embrace of diversity invariably yields.

Referring to the Arabs under illegal Israeli occupation, Tarazi writes:

> 3.5 million Palestinian Christians and Muslims, are denied the same political and civil rights as Jews. These Palestinians must drive on separate roads, in cars bearing distinctive license plates, and only to and from designated Palestinian areas. It is illegal for a Palestinian to drive a car with an Israeli license

plate. These Palestinians, as non-Jews, neither qualify for Israeli citizenship nor have the right to vote in Israeli elections. In South Africa, such an allocation of rights and privileges based on ethnic or religious affiliation was called apartheid. In Israel, it is called the Middle East's only democracy.

Tarazi, reflecting a small but growing body of Palestinian opinion, is tentatively proposing an end to legalized discrimination and daily humiliation through the creation of a single binational state, endowed with a pluralist constitution reflecting the multifaith diversity of the various groups inhabiting the Holy Land.

From a Jewish perspective the flaw in this "one-state solution" is glaring, and Foxman has no trouble spotting it: "Mr. Tarazi's proposal is the latest of many efforts by Palestinian officials to subvert the existence of Israel in the garb of victimhood. In the old days it was manifest in an outright rejection of Israel's right to exist—which Hamas and Islamic Jihad continue to advocate. Today, we see it in Mr. Tarazi's cynical proposal for one state, which of course would be the end of a Jewish state in Israel by overwhelming a Jewish majority through numbers."

Israel, in Foxman's analysis, literally cannot exist without a Jewish majority, because a Jewish majority is what constitutes Israel as a Jewish state. Israel is Israel only insofar as it is a Jewish state with a Jewish majority, which means that non-Jews on the occupied West Bank and in Israel proper, survivors of Jewish ethnic cleansing, are at best irrelevant to Israel's identity and at worst a demographic time-bomb, capable of bringing about national annihilation. Israel will come to an end the moment Arabs outnumber Jews.

The ADL's director and chief spokesman is giving us a succinct demonstration of Jewish hypocrisy. In Israel Jews have formed a Jewish ethnostate for themselves and allow no one except Jews to immigrate into it, not even the Palestinian Arabs they ejected in 1948, while in the West they campaign for multiculturalism, affirmative action, and Third World immigration. American Jews, Foxman and the ADL prominent among them, teach Whites the need to "embrace diversity," that is, to willingly accept dispossession as a moral obligation. Yet they have no desire to see their fellow Jews do the same in Israel, and they will dismiss any suggestion that Israeli Jews follow the path of equality and pluralism as a "cynical proposal" for Israel's destruction.

The Jewish state has ample room for millions of Jewish immigrants, none with any legal claim to land in Palestine. It therefore obviously has room for more Arabs. But no American Zionist wants his co-religionists to become a minority in Israel. "Our diversity is our strength" is just an infantile, quasi-Orwellian slogan applicable only to Whites, not to the slogan's inventors. ("Our disunity is our unity" would be an Orwellian slogan; "our diversity is our strength" comes close.)

We should never tire of identifying Jewish hypocrisy on racial issues and never fear repetition. Foxman is the leader of an avowedly anti-racialist organization. Promoting racial diversity is his job, and whatever we may think of the ADL's mission, no one could deny that Abraham Foxman and the ADL work hard and work effectively at nurturing anti-White discrimination and racial balkanization in the United States. And they have a real record of solid accomplishment, including membership in the long list of Jewish organizations and Jewish politicians that opened American borders to the Third World in 1965.

In this, as Kevin MacDonald documents, Jews were pursuing their own racial interests at our expense. A multiracial society strengthens Jews by weakening the dominant Gentile culture and diffusing power among a series of competing groups, with Jews assuming a leadership role within the squabbling alien nation created by non-White demographics. All talk from Jews of "diversity" and "equality" and "racial justice" is camouflage concealing their hidden agenda, as well as *ad hoc* propaganda concocted to discourage the Euro-American majority from acting as a cohesive group with legitimate interests of its own.

Jews, it is true, can become tearily emotional when they speak of racial diversity, as though, gifted with special spiritual insight, they see in expanding non-White populations a moral progression away from primitive race loyalty and toward a new age of enlightened racelessness. "If you believe," the neo-conservative Ben Wattenberg has written, ". . . that the American drama is being played out toward a purpose, then the non-Europeanization of America is heartening news of an almost transcendental quality."

Yet we know for certain that such eloquent professions of anti-racialism are a sham, representing only a Jewish tactic, not a genuine belief. That is the most important lesson which broad Jewish support for Zionism teaches. If Wattenberg had also extolled the "almost transcendental quality" of some future dejudaization of Israel, we would be forced to concede his sincerity. Since he is in fact a Zionist, we can justly dismiss him as a fraud and accurately label him a political enemy, as we can all Jews who exhibit the same self-interested double standard.

It is clear that no Jew can be at once a principled anti-racialist and a principled supporter of Israel, and since most Jews are both anti-racialists and Zionists, we can safely conclude that most Jews are unprincipled hypocrites, claiming a purported moral quality—anti-racialism—that they manifestly do not possess.

Lying back of the proposed one-state solution to the Mideast conflict is Zionism's nightmare scenario, the return of the indigenous Palestinians expelled from their homes at the birth of the Jewish state. Israel was created by an act of the United Nations in 1947. It is therefore a legitimate nation, at least if we accept the UN as the arbiter of national legitimacy. Israel has, however, an unusual legal status that distinguishes it from all other legitimate nations. Subsequent UN resolutions, specifically Resolution 194 (December 1948) and Resolution 273 (May 1949), made Israel's admission to the world body contingent on its willingness to allow Palestinian refugees "to return to their homes." General Assembly Resolution 194, which has been reaffirmed annually, is the main legal basis for what Palestinians call the Right of Return.

Somewhere between 500,000 and 800,000 Arabs were forcibly ejected from Palestine during Israel's War of Independence, and they and their descendants, now numbering about three million and strewn about the Middle East, are entitled to return under international law. Thus Israeli Jews, alone among the nations of the world, are legally obligated to "embrace diversity," though it is an obligation which they have not the slightest intention of fulfilling.

When Abraham Foxman angrily dismisses the one-state solution, he is not merely rejecting diversity as a Euro-American nationalist would; he is rejecting diversity despite the existence of an international obligation to accept it. Multiracialists insist that Whites have a moral obligation to become minorities in their own nations, but only for Israeli Jews is the alleged moral imperative of majority self-dissolution coupled with a legal mandate.

Should Israel acknowledge its legal obligations, accepting a single binational state and the Right of Return as matters of selfless principle, Jews in Israel would soon find themselves facing the same demographic threat that their Diaspora brethren have engineered for us. That so many Zionist Jews in the West remain anti-White activists under this unusual set of circumstances, that they continue defending an explicitly Jewish state while daily thinking up new schemes to further deracialize their host populations, requires a brazen racial chauvinism which only a race that regards hypocrisy as its birthright could ever practice.

http://library.flawlesslogic.com/orientalism.htm

Ruling the World
by Proxy

Mahathir Mohamad, the former Malaysian prime minister, announced last month that "Jews rule this world by proxy. They get others to fight and die for them." The Israeli writer Uri Avnery voiced a similar opinion back in April: "America controls the world, we control America. Never before have Jews exerted such an immense influence on the center of world power."

Both men were thinking chiefly of the invasion of Iraq, an event that has clearly revealed how US Mideast policy revolves around Israeli interests, to the detriment of American interests and at the cost, in this case, of the American occupiers now dying daily, nineteen just yesterday.

Jewish neo-conservatives have long argued that "the road to Jerusalem goes through Baghdad." The removal of Saddam's Baathist regime, the strongest Arab supporter of the Palestinians, would strengthen Israel in her dealings with the Arab world, inducing Palestinian negotiators to accept a dictated peace on Israel's terms and beginning an incremental process of Mideast regime change that would gradually surround the Jewish state with pliant neighbors. That was the neo-conservative theory, and only time will tell whether it was correct. In the interim young Americans and young Britons will continue to die in the expectation that their blood will eventually benefit Israel, the true homeland of the Perle-Wolfowitz cabal that engineered the invasion. (They actually call themselves a "cabal," it is worth noting.)

In discussing Jewish instigation of the ongoing Iraq war, we can rely on facts that are not in dispute. It is, for example, an acknowledged fact, reported by mainstream news sources, that influential Jews inside the Bush administration furnished much of the disinformation that justified the invasion. Frustrated by the failure of conventional intelligence agencies to find credible proof of a threatening Iraqi weapons program, Paul Wolfowitz and Douglas Feith, both Jews, established the Office of Special Plans, headed by Abram Shulsky, also Jewish. This *ad hoc* intelligence operation, set up inside the Pentagon for the express purpose of supplying a rationale for war, found what they were looking for: evidence of what Wolfowitz would memorably call Saddam's "arsenal of terror," smoking-gun evidence which the real intelligence community had been unable to discover for the simple reason that it did not exist. As Vince Cannistraro, former CIA chief of counter-terrorism, complained: "Their methods are vicious. The politicization of intelligence is pandemic, and deliberate disinformation is being promoted."

The political strength that enabled American Zionists to convince the American people to believe their fabrications does not itself amount to "rul[ing] this world by proxy," but it certainly does represent, in Uri Avnery's words, "an immense influence on the center of world power."

This immense influence is protected by informal rules that mandate the stigmatizing of any non-Jew who openly names and criticizes it. Condoleezza Rice accordingly called Mahathir Mohamad's comments "hateful" and "outrageous." That is, of course, the formulaic language normally deployed to dismiss any criticism of Jewish power, and it presupposes that the speaker of the hatefully outrageous comments in question disapproves of what he is attempting to describe. The prime minister was not praising Jews for their role in shaping American Mideast policy; he was describing their power to "get others to fight and die for them." Because he opposes that power, he becomes "hateful." Natan (Anatoly) Sharansky, former deputy prime minister of Israel, does not oppose Jewish power, but on one important issue he and Mahathir Mohamad are in agreement. "Israel," he wrote recently, "has few strategic assets as critical as American Jewry. The fact that the world's leading superpower is a steadfast ally of Israel is due in large measure to this proud and activist community."

Since Sharansky approves of Jewish political power and hopes that it will persist, he cannot, by the standards that govern the adjective, be called "hateful." No canned outrage will be forthcoming from Condoleezza Rice, even though Sharansky unwittingly corroborated a traditional charge of anti-Semites. If American Jews are indeed a critical "strategic asset" that ensures, in large measure, steadfast American support for Israel, then by the same token it is fair to call American Jews, in large measure, an alien fifth column, acting on behalf of another nation, indifferent to the welfare of the nation to which they nominally profess allegiance. Admiral Thomas Moorer once remarked: "If the American people understood what a grip those people have on our government, they would rise up in arms. Our citizens don't have any idea what goes on." Sharansky was speaking from the perspective of an Israeli Jew who naturally wants this grip on the center of world power to remain.

Sharansky's language also has the advantage of greater precision. It is not exactly true that Jews rule the world by proxy. If that were the case, the Palestinians would have been forcibly ejected from the West Bank decades ago. It is, however, exactly true that Jewish Zionists, as a major strategic asset of another nation, form a powerful activist community working within the United States on behalf of Israel, and it is beyond dispute that one of their goals was the displacement of Iraq's old government by a new government more amenable to their designs. Put simply, if there were no activist Jews influencing political decisions in Washington, there would be no American and British forces in Iraq. Natan Sharansky would likely agree.

Your attitude to "this proud and activist community" will thus depend on how you evaluate their work. If you favor an Israel-centered Mideast policy, then you should applaud their efforts and revel in their latest success. But if it bothers you to see Americans dying daily in Iraq for someone else's benefit, then you have good cause for anger.

National Vanguard (online), April 11, 2003

JEWS, ISLAM, &
ORIENTALISM

In Western history the Spanish Reconquista stands as an important landmark. Spain had once belonged to Islam, but with Reconquest the long Islamic intrusion which had begun in 711 was brought to an end, apparently decisively. From a Christian perspective the Reconquista was the gradual expulsion, beginning in the eleventh century and ending in the fifteenth, of Muslim unbelievers from the southwestern corner of Christendom; from a racialist perspective it was a literal culture-war of Europeans against Moors, waged by Spaniards, Frenchmen and Portuguese, the chivalry of White Europe. In simple political terms, comprehensible to anyone regardless of political affiliation, it was the end of foreign domination. Southern Spain had been under Muslim occupation for almost eight hundred years, and with the fall in 1492 of Granada, the last Muslim kingdom in Spain, the Reconquista was complete. Under Ferdinand and Isabella, the most successful chapter in Spain's history was just beginning.

Three centuries later the German-Jewish poet Heinrich Heine (1797-1856) would envision this epochal Reconquista much differently: "On the tower [in Cordova] where the muezzin called to prayer there is now the melancholy tolling of church bells. On the steps where the [Muslim] faithful sang the words of the Prophet, tonsured monks are acting out their lugubrious charades." For Heine, Islamic Spain—here represented by formerly Muslim Cordova, reconquered in 1236—had fallen victim to "the dark tricks of history," and the Reconquista, far from being a righteous European triumph over an alien and expansionist adversary, marked a terrible cultural disaster. The Spain that emerged from her national victories was spiritually impoverished and intellectually desolate, filled with the sterile ceremonies of mindless Catholicism. Spain, in short, was better off Islamic. The wrong side had won.

Heine's lines are from his poem "Almansor," which was based on his play of the same title. They are quoted in Martin Kramer's introduction to *The Jewish Discovery of Islam* (Tel Aviv: The Moshe Dayan Center for Middle Eastern and African Studies, 1999), a collection of essays discussing Jewish contributions to the European investigation of the Muslim world. Kramer, the collection's editor, treats Heine's poetic lament for Muslim losses as an example of European Jewry's "heightened empathy and sympathy for Islam," but another motive is also clear. Heine sympathized with the Muslim invaders of Europe because he disliked Europeans. His enemy's enemy was his friend. Empathy for Islam was hostility to Christian Europe. Thus at the end of "Almansor" the poem's Muslim protagonist, though baptized a Christian (a formality that Heine himself would undergo in 1825), feels the growing anger of Cordova's famous cathedral, once a mosque in the happy days of Islamic occupation, and dreams of seeing the desecrated mosque crash vengefully down upon the Spanish congregants below, "while the Christian Gods shriek and wail."

Kramer, an expatriate American Jew who works at Tel Aviv University's Moshe Dayan Center, planned *The Jewish Discovery of Islam* as a Jewish response to the Palestinian literary critic Edward Said's poisonously influential *Orientalism* (New York: Vintage, 1978), easily the most destructive anti-Western book of the past half-century. The object of Said's attack was the academic discipline of Orientalism, the study of the East and its various cultures, especially Islam. European scholarship, he argued, had defined and essentialized Islam as a hostile and culturally inferior Other, while ignoring the profound interconnections between East and West. Orientalism, an expression of the West's arrogant Eurocentrism, had created a distorted representation of the East's inferiority and then proceeded to justify and extend European colonialism on the basis of the self-interested simulacrum it had produced. "Orientalism," Said wrote, "was ultimately a political vision of reality whose structure promoted the difference between the familiar (Europe, the West, 'us') and the strange (the Orient, the East, 'them')," and in an oft-quoted pronouncement he alleged that "every European, in what he could say about the Orient, was consequently a racist, an imperialist, and almost totally ethnocentric" (*Orientalism*, pp. 43, 68).

Said's Orientalism has become the bible of fashionable Third Worldism and the central document of postcolonial studies, which it did much to spawn. As a result of its remarkable influence the term "Orientalism," which once denoted an arcane discipline specializing in esoteric languages and odd religious practices, has become a powerful slur, not much different from "racism." And like anti-racialism, Saidian anti-Orientalism denies our right to see the world through our own eyes, to see the Islamic world as indeed Other, substantially different from the West in ways that traditional Orientalism had enumerated. If today we view the *burqa*-shrouded women of Afghanistan as symptoms of a strange and primitive culture, then we are guilty of Eurocentric Orientalism, because we immorally claim for ourselves the right to judge the Muslim Other by our own standards.

Said, though wrongly labeled an anti-Semite for his criticism of Israel, carefully avoided distinguishing Jewish from non-Jewish Orientalists. All were European and therefore all equally "racist." Kramer's book is an attempt to remedy that deficiency. Jewish Orientalists, Kramer explains, did not suffer from the essentialist, polarizing prejudices of their non-Jewish colleagues: "The work of Jewish orientalists—liberals and Marxists, Zionists and assimilationists, believers and atheists—subverted the idea that East and West were polar opposites. Much of Europe debated whether the Jews belonged to one or the other; Jews replied that the question itself lacked validity. The work of Jewish orientalists at every turn challenged the tendency to interpret Islam or Judaism *sui generis*, and their message was remarkably uniform: Islamic history (like Jewish history) can be subjected to the same analytical tools as Europe's; Europe's civilization rests also on Islamic (and Jewish) foundations; Islam (like Judaism) is no anachronism, but undergoes constant adaptation, and would accommodate even European modernity. Jews urged European respect for peoples bearing cultures of extra-European origin, precisely because the Jews were the most vulnerable of these peoples, residing as they did in the very center of Europe." Jews, in other words, were *de facto* anti-Orientalists well before Edward Said launched his attack on Eurocentric Orientalism.

All of this will sound familiar to readers of Kevin MacDonald's *Culture of Critique*, which documents how ostensibly neutral Jewish scholarship has often served a hidden racial agenda. Jewish scholars wrote sympathetically about Islam in order to attack Europe indirectly. While maintaining the pretense of disinterested objectivity they sought to dismantle categories that helped Europeans to define themselves, and by challenging generalizations about Muslims they hoped to inhibit similar generalizations about Jews. Their principal target was Europe's confident belief in its cultural superiority, and insofar as Christian Europe defined itself in contrast to Islam, they would attack Europe by elevating its opposite and by challenging the boundaries between East and West and Islam and Christendom that formed parts of Europe's insufferable self-image. We can think of this, keeping in mind the example of Heine's sublimated hatred, as restrained aggression expressed through a calculated sanitizing of Islam, with the aim of undermining Europe's identity and eliminating its suspicion of the Muslim outsider. As Heinrich Heine placed his own racial aggression in the thoughts and experiences of the fictional Muslim Almansor ben Abdullah, so Jewish scholarship concealed its anti-European aggression in the learned pages of sympathetic studies of Islam.

Kramer is bold in assessing the effects of this intellectual subversion: "The respect for Islam that Jews had done so much to disseminate not only survived in Europe but served as the basis for Europe's tolerance of Muslim minorities after the war. The mosque-like synagogues erected by Jewish communities in the nineteenth century prepared Europe to accept the real mosques which Muslim communities erected across the continent in the twentieth." Bernard Lewis, the most distinguished of modern Jewish Orientalists, recently predicted in *Die Welt* that "Europe will be Islamic by the end of the century"; for this demographic catastrophe Kramer claims credit on behalf of Islamophile Jewish scholarship. That may be too great a burden for the musty tomes of half-forgotten Jewish Orientalists to bear, but Jewish promotion of Islam does provide at least a partial explanation for the massive loss of European will that has allowed the growing Muslim invasion once again assailing the continent, this time without (as yet) any significant resistance. And there can be no doubt that the West's old view of Islam as hostile and alien, a reasonable response to a long history of Muslim invasions, has been almost entirely eradicated. When

NATO elected to empower Muslim terrorists in Kosovo by bombing Serbs in Belgrade, that nominally Western decision powerfully signaled the breakdown of our former cultural self-image. Any reflexive assumption that Serbs are Europeans and Muslims alien outsiders had vanished. For this, if Kramer's analysis is correct, we can blame Jews.

French president Jacques Chirac has spoken of "a Europe whose roots are as much Muslim as Christian." The idea is bizarre, and traditional scholarship conceptualized French national history in precisely contrary terms. France was spared the Islamic invasion that swept across Spain by Charles ("the Hammer") Martel's victory in 732 at the Battle of Poitiers; France could become French only because she had first defeated Islam. Ideas, like people, have a lineage, and we can be certain that Jacques Chirac's fantastic belief in Europe's Muslim roots cannot be traced back to the polarizing interpretations of Eurocentric Orientalists. It is a subversive Jewish idea that has made its way into the conventional mind of a politician, much as the widespread myth of Muslim religious tolerance—an idea George W. Bush is fond of mentioning in his many homilies on Islam the religion of peace—was (to quote Bernard Lewis) "invented by Jews in nineteenth-century Europe as a reproach to Christians . . ." Both ideas are false, but it was once useful for Jews to circulate them.

We should take note of the philo-Semitic environment in which Jews worked to subvert Europe's cultural self-understanding. Among the Gentile Orientalists who numerically dominated the discipline in the 1800s, the most prominent White racialist was the brilliant Ernest Renan (1823–92), who believed that Jews were Europeans, which is to say that Renan was not much of a racialist at all. "Jewish scholars," Kramer writes, "were not to be regarded as Semitic specimens, but as fellow Europeans, who could participate as intellectual equals in Europe's discovery of Islam." The subversive, Islamophile Orientalism of Jewish scholars flourished in an academic environment characterized by low levels of anti-Semitism, but clearly this racial tolerance did not emotionally bind these Jews to the West. In the academic history Kramer outlines tolerance was not repaid with gratitude and cultural loyalty; it simply afforded Jews a position of safety from which to pursue their racial interests and launch their campaign against Europe. A scarcity of anti-Semitism is always an open invitation to Jewish misbehavior, because it frees Jews from inspection of their motives.

Kramer himself is no tolerant Islamophile, and he feels none of the "heightened empathy and sympathy for Islam" that he honors. He is an anti-Muslim neo-conservative, and like all neo-conservatives he advocates a hard American stance against the Muslim world, including the bombing of Iraqi cities and the destruction ("democratization") of anti-Zionist Muslim nations, all for the betterment of Israel. "The moment America's commitment to Israel seems diminished in Arab eyes," he argues elsewhere, "the region is destined to spiral into war." Kramer praises the tolerant Jewish Orientalists of bygone centuries because they are safely dead, and he has no intention of following their example. In their covert race war against Western civilization Jews once benefited from sanitizing Islam and from making the strange seem familiar, yet retaining the old model of Jewish Orientalism would provide no advantages today. Islam has very few virtues, but anti-Semitism is, luckily, among them. Muslims hate the West, but they hate Jews and Zionism even more. The recent Jewish discovery of deep, apparently ineradicable Muslim anti-Semitism has convinced neo-conservative Jews like Martin Kramer that in our era any "heightened empathy and sympathy for Islam" would be a dangerous mistake. Kramer can boast of how, in his opinion, Jewish scholarship helped bring millions of violent Muslims back into Europe, but he knows that today Muslims are a formidable enemy of Jews and the Jewish state, and so he and his fellow neo-conservatives have assumed a new role as truth-telling opponents of Islamism and vigilant defenders of the West, a West whose center of gravity is located in Tel Aviv.

http://library.flawlesslogic.com/orientalism.htm

ABROGATED VERSES
IN THE KORAN*

"Let there be no compulsion in religion; truth stands out clear from error" (Sura 2.256). Apologists for Islam often quote this verse, and most Westerners, unfamiliar with the Koran and imagining that it must obey the same theological logic as the Christian Bible, assume that Islamic scripture mandates religious toleration toward non-Muslims. That assumption is inaccurate.

The Koran includes many abrogated verses, called *mansukh*, and abrogating verses, *nasikh*; the latter cancel the former, rendering them invalid, though they nevertheless remain in the Koran and are deceptively quoted, for Western consumption, as though they still represented genuine Islamic beliefs. *Nasikh* and *mansukh* are legion: Of the Koran's 114 *suras* (chapters), only 43 are without abrogated or abrogating verses. That is naturally surprising, and so unexpected that few Westerners are aware that significant segments of the Koran have been theologically annulled. Mohammed's non-Muslim contemporaries were just as surprised.

How does one know, when two verses are contradictory, which is abrogated and which is abrogating? It is a question of date: Later texts abrogate earlier texts whenever there are inconsistencies between them. The Koranic verses that teach tolerance and peace, in particular those

---

* This text was co-authored by Irmin Vinson and an anonymous French author. It is Vinson's translation, with extensive revisions, of an anonymous French text that he found online. If you can provide the author and source of the original French text, please contact the editor at editor@counter-currents.com.

that prohibit compulsion in religion, are among the earliest of Mohammed's many revelations and are thus liable to abrogation, whenever Allah felt the inclination to revoke his immutable word. Although Islam, unlike Judaism and Christianity, received its revelation from a single person within a short period of time, roughly twenty years, Mohammed was nonetheless able to impose upon his followers the implausible belief that the inerrant Muslim God had routinely changed his mind.

The pacific, tolerant message of Sura 2.256 reflects the historical circumstances of its composition. Islam was still then decidedly a minority faith and Mohammed and his small band of followers, in Medina and surrounded by non-Muslim enemies, were threatened with destruction. The early Koran of necessity presented religious tolerance as a divine command because nascent Islam had not yet acquired the physical power to compel conversion: "The Apostle had not been given permission to fight or allowed to shed blood . . . he had simply been ordered to call men to God, endure insult, and forgive the ignorant" (*Ibn Ishaq, Sirat Rasul Allah*).

But when Islam became powerful, Allah's eternal message changed. Islam could now "call people by the sword"—that is, compel conversion—and accordingly "verses of the sword" were conveniently revealed to the Prophet, verses that sanction and indeed command conversion of the Infidel by armed violence, which historically would be Islam's preferred method. Sura 2.256 was thus abrogated by a later verse, composed after Mohammed had begun to prepare his new Muslim empire for Jihad against the non-Muslim world: "Slay the idolaters wherever you find them, and take them, and confine them, and lie in wait for them at every place of ambush" (Sura 9.5). This "verse of the sword" not only abrogates 2.256, but also abrogates well over a hundred earlier verses that formerly taught peace and tolerance toward non-believers.

Only the later, abrogating verse now represents authentic Muslim teaching.

Islam: "Religion of Peace"

"Those that make war against Allah and His apostle and spread disorder in the land shall be slain or crucified or have their hands and feet cut off on alternate sides, or be banished from the land. They shall be held up to shame in this world and sternly punished in the hereafter." (Sura 5.33)

"O believers, take not Jews and Christians as friends; they are friends of each other. Whoso of you makes them his friends is one of them. Allah guides not the people of the evildoers." (Sura 5.51)

"Allah revealed His will to the angels, saying: 'I shall be with you. Give courage to the believers. I shall cast terror into the hearts of the infidels. Strike off their heads, strike off the very tips of their fingers!' That was because they defied Allah and His apostle. He that defies Allah and his apostle shall be sternly punished by Allah." (Sura 8.12–13)

"In order that Allah may separate the pure from the impure, put all the impure ones [i.e. non-Muslims] one on top of another in a heap and cast them into hell. They will have been the ones to have lost." (Sura 8.37)

"And fight them until there is no more *fitnah* (disbelief and polytheism, i.e. worshipping others besides Allah) and the religion (worship) will all be for Allah alone (in the whole world). But if they cease (worshipping others besides Allah) then certainly, Allah is All-Seer of what they do." (Sura 8.39).

"Muster against them [i.e. non-Muslims] all the men and cavalry at your command, so that you may strike terror into the enemy of Allah and your enemy, and others besides them who are unknown to you but known to Allah." (Sura 8.60)

"O Prophet, urge on the believers to fight. If there be twenty of you, patient men, they will overcome two hundred; if there be a hundred of you, they will overcome a thousand unbelievers, for they are a people who understand not." (Sura 8.65)

"It is not for any Prophet to have prisoners until he make wide slaughter in the land." (Sura 8.67).

"Fight those who believe not in Allah and the Last Day and do not forbid what Allah and His Messenger have forbidden—such men as practice not the religion of truth, being of those who have been given the Book [i.e. Jews and Christians]—until they pay the tribute out of hand and have been humbled." (Sura 9.29)

"If you do not go to war, He will punish you sternly, and will replace you by other men." (Sura 9.39)

"Prophet, make war on the unbelievers and the hypocrites, and deal harshly with them. Hell shall be their home: an evil fate." (Sura 9.73)

"They [i.e. faithful Muslims] will fight for the cause of Allah, they will slay and be slain." (Sura 9.111)

"O believers, fight the unbelievers who are near to you, and let them find in you a harshness, and know that Allah is with the godfearing." (Sura 9.123)

"When We resolve to raze a city, We first give warning to those of its people who live in comfort. If they persist in sin, judgment is irrevocably passed, and We destroy it utterly." (Sura 17.16)

"We have destroyed many a sinful nation and replaced them by other men. And when they felt Our Might they took to their heels and fled. They were told: 'Do not run away. Return to your comforts and to your dwellings. You shall be questioned all.' 'Woe betide us, we have done wrong' was their reply. And this they kept repeating until We mowed them down and put out their light." (Sura 21.11–15)

"When you meet the unbelievers in the battlefield strike off their heads and, when you have laid them low, bind your captives firmly. Then grant them their freedom or take a ransom from them, until war shall lay down her burdens." (Sura 47.4)

"Mohammed is Allah's apostle. Those who follow him are ruthless to the unbelievers but merciful to one another." (Sura 48.29)

"May the hands of Abu Lahab [Mohammed's uncle, who had refused to embrace Islam] perish! Nothing shall his wealth and gains avail him. He shall be burnt in a flaming fire, and his wife, laden with firewood, shall have a rope of fiber around her neck!" (Sura 111.1–5)

http://library.flawlesslogic.com/verses.htm

The Lessons of Madrid

In the wake of the Madrid bombings of March 11, 2004, which left 202 dead and almost 1,700 wounded, the head of France's armed forces, Henri Bentegeat, called Al-Qaeda "a hydra with many heads.... If we catch one head, there will be others."

General Bentegeat's metaphor was intended to capture the diffuse character of Islamic terrorism, which is not centralized in a single hierarchical network but instead localized in small cells, many of them spread throughout the West, where they work toward common Islamic objectives, like blowing up trains.

His metaphor was also a PC circumlocution, an elegant way of obfuscating a glaring and deadly problem in multiracial demography, part of what Welsh actor John Rhys-Davies has called the "demographic catastrophe happening in Europe that nobody wants to talk about."

Bentegeat really meant, concretely, that Europe has far too many Muslims who share the ideals of the Muslim terrorists responsible for the Madrid bombings. If you arrest one group of Muslim terrorists, there will still remain a deep reservoir of militant Muslims who can take up where their predecessors left off. There are, for example, over 100,000 Muslims in Madrid alone, a dark body of multiracial diversity large enough to spawn dozens of new hydra heads, even if the Spanish police manage to kill off the current hydra.

Bentegeat's own nation is dedicated, like most of the West, to non-enforcement of immigration law and ritual celebration of the resulting racial balkanization. It is afflicted with over five million Muslims, along with a rich culture of Muslim crime and violence unparalleled in Europe. Large sections of many French cities have become Maghrebi versions of Detroit, and a Muslim terror cell in France, the Servants of Allah the Powerful and Wise, has just threatened the French government over its secularist attempt to ban Muslim headscarves from public schools: "With this headscarf law, you have participated in an unjust aggression. You have decided on your own to put yourself on the list of Islam's worst enemies."

As with many racial issues, it is useful to step back from the details of current events and look clearly at the obvious. The best way to stop the spread of radical Islam in the West is to stop the importation of Muslims. Islamic terror thrives on open borders. A valuable tautology: Not all Muslims are terrorists, but all Muslim terrorists are Muslims. If you want more Muslim terrorists, import more Muslims. If you don't want more Muslim terrorists, close your borders against Muslims.

No reasonable person could deny those self-evident truths, but the powerful dogmas of multiracialism inhibit anyone with mainstream pretensions from openly saying them. Hence General Bentegeat's imprecise talk of self-replicating "hydra heads" of Islamic terror, when he should have identified the lethal threat posed by millions of Third World Muslims spread across Europe.

This pattern of PC obfuscation is common throughout the West. On March 17, 2004, Ken Livingstone, London's multiracialist mayor, spoke of the inevitability of a terror attack of Madrid-like proportions against his city: "Given that some are prepared to give their own lives, it would be inconceivable that someone does not get through to London." Mayor Livingstone is not worried that recent Swedish immigrants are likely to kill British citizens in the name of Allah. He fears that Muslims will. And of course the amorphous "someone" he mentions doesn't need to "get through to London," since this someone and his co-religionists already live there, as the result of an immigration policy that Livingstone himself aggressively supports. London, or "Londonistan" in the parlance of both European police forces and Islamic jihadists, now has a large enough supply of Muslim militants that it regularly exports them around the globe. Islam did not descend upon London like toxic manna from heaven; two million Muslims were imported into Britain through a consciously anti-racialist immigration policy that all mainstream British political parties defend.

An obvious but generally unacknowledged truth concealed by the War on Terror is that we are rarely threatened by Muslims until they arrive on our shores. We in the West are not seriously endangered by radical Islam in (say) Pakistan, though the Pakistanis are, paradoxically, endangered by radical Islam in Britain, which now exports its own homegrown jihadists, indoctrinated in Londonistan, to their country, along with several others. Tony Blair's multiracial Cool Britannia is both an importer and an exporter of Muslim fanatics.

Did Spain become safer because her outgoing government supported the Anglo-American invasion of Iraq? Would Spain be safer today if previous Spanish governments had prohibited Muslim immigration from North Africa? Was old White London more or less at risk of Islamic terror than modern Londonistan? Does the presence of seven million Muslims on American soil increase or decrease the likelihood of further Muslim terror attacks against Americans? If their number doubles, will Americans be safer or more at risk? These are not complicated questions, and we all know the answers. Securing your own national borders is a better protection against terrorism than violating someone else's.

Over half of the rapists in Denmark are Muslims, and

most of their victims are native-born White women, often young teens subjected to violent gang rapes. Multiracialists in Europe shrug off unpleasant facts of this sort as the price of celebrating such a rich abundance of diversity.

But they may find exploding trains more difficult to rationalize. More than any other event the rise, over the last decade, of Islamic terror within the West has demolished, for any sensible observer, the bizarre multiculturalist proposition that celebrating the cultural differences of incompatible peoples can be a source of national strength.

Multiracialism tells us that it would be very wicked ("racist") for majority-White nations to exclude any group of non-White immigrants. The steady flow of non-Whites from the Third World into the West, present and future Muslim terrorists among them, thus becomes a moral imperative, an imperative that only far-right "racists" refuse to acknowledge. Which is another way of saying that racialism is simple common sense, and that anti-racialism is Islamic terror's most reliable ally.

http://library.flawlesslogic.com/madrid.htm

WAGNER &
MULTIRACIALISM

In his analysis of Nikolaus Lehnhoff's production of *Der Fliegende Holländer* (*The Flying Dutchman*) Michael Polignano mentions that "desecrating Wagner...is something of an industry in post-World War II Germany."[1] The recent Stuttgart version of Wagner's four-opera Ring Cycle, available on DVD for anyone who wants to waste money, provides a good illustration. The following is an excerpt from an online review:

> In *Rheingold* the gods don't ascend into Valhalla, they go down into the basement. In *Walküre*, Siegmund doesn't pull the sword out of a tree (there isn't any), but from Sieglinde's bodice, and it is embarrassing to watch the two of them, with flailing arms and legs, in simulated coupling on top of a table. The Valkyries are high-heeled tarts with paper wings, and occasionally during *Ride of the Valkyries* what looks like a mummy (representing a fallen hero) is dragged across the stage. At the end of this opera Wotan doesn't look at Brünnhilde except via a TV set (which he operates with a remote)—even though she is right in front of him on the upper stage level. There's no "magic fire" except for five small candles which she lights herself. In *Siegfried*, after watching Mime masturbate in scene three of act one, the hero (who has "Sieg Fried" printed on

---

[1] Michael J. Polignano, "Wagner: Desecrated but not Defeated," in *Taking Our Own Side*, ed. Greg Johnson (San Francisco: Counter-Currents Publishing, 2010).

his T-shirt) discovers Brünnhilde in what appears to be a kitchen which happens to have a bed in it. As both are not small singers, it is rather comical to watch their mating ritual, reminiscent of a PBS nature documentary.[2]

Productions of this sort are usually surrounded by self-serving artspeak: They're cutting-edge, daring, disturbing, groundbreaking, subversive, etc. These claims of cutting-edge boldness are quite obviously untrue, but there is a good chance that anti-Wagnerian directors believe them. If you imagine a Pythonesque Twit who delusively visualizes himself as an avant-garde artist, you'll have captured the core personality of Wagner desecraters like Nikolaus Lehnhoff. In modern Germany an authentically Wagnerian Ring would be genuinely bold and subversive, since the primary purpose of all postwar German governments has been to de-ethnicize and de-racialize their citizenry. Because artistic recollections of ancient Nordic mythology could potentially do the opposite, anti-Wagnerians carefully degrade or excise Wagner's Nordic mythos. Thus in the Stuttgart *Rheingold* Valhalla is located in a basement, rather than in the sky, and the gods enter Valhalla not by crossing a rainbow bridge but by descending in an old elevator. Clearly this production is not a modernization for the purpose of illuminating hidden dimensions of Wagner's drama; it expresses unmistakable aggression, burning hatred for what the real Ring Cycle represents.

For the Stuttgart Ring four separate artistic teams were assigned the task of wrecking an opera according to their own inclinations, and although each team produced its own particular form of desecration marked by significant stylistic differences, an intense hostility to Wagner's my-

---

[2] http://classicalcdreview.com/DVDVIDEO25.html

thology was the feature they ended up sharing in common. All arrived independently at a single anti-mythological focus for their loathing. Anti-Wagnerians do not, as Polignano points out, engage in random desecration, since this aggressive demythologizing, practiced in varying degrees by all anti-Wagnerian productions, is ideologically systematic. Everything that seems threatening to the antinational German establishment is a target. The music survives unscathed, but the Wagnerian mythology that once informed it is trashed or eliminated in deliberate acts of cultural ethnic cleansing. The purportedly "daring" Stuttgart Ring is really no more daring than a state-circulated anti-racism leaflet or a bureaucratic document outlining changes in the tax code. All are instruments of state power.

In George Orwell's dystopian account of the future, history can be eradicated by a state-orchestrated program of mandatory forgetting, because history is intangible and unable to defend itself. Having no solid existence, it survives only in books and in cultural memory, and in *1984* history can be changed or destroyed by the totalitarian state simply by rewriting or destroying the books in which it is documented, in the expectation that memory will wither soon after and that new memories can be artificially produced to replace the old. Enemies of state power and state ideology can be eliminated ("vaporized") from history, as though they had never lived, and the past can be continually reshaped to serve Ingsoc's latest political objectives.

In practice, however, anti-racialists have generally adopted a different tactic, preferring to hollow out old forms, emptying them of their original content but preserving a debased semblance of the originals. The intention—to control the past—is the same, though the method is different. There are in fact certain cultural monuments, like Wagnerian opera in Germany, that cannot be easily eradicated or dropped down the memory hole. Although Wagner is perceived by anti-national Germans as an old enemy, and hated accordingly, he is an enemy who cannot be forgotten. He occupies too prominent a position in the musical pantheon of the past. For dedicated multiracialists his most threatening art must therefore be aggressively reproduced in misshapen travesties of his original vision.

When thinking about these travesties it's hard to know whether anger or laughter is the more appropriate response. Of the two, however, I'd pick laughter. Multiracialism's hatred for a long-dead composer of operas must surely indicate weakness and unease. If you wanted to recruit a revolutionary organization, middle-aged opera fans would be a poor demographic to select. Yet German multiracialists evidently fear rotund ladies wearing winged helmets performing in traditional Wagnerian operas before placid audiences, because they fear *anything* that challenges their dogmas. Such fear does not suggest real confidence. Anti-national Germans are literally afraid of operas.

Nowhere in the West has multiracialism ever been presented as a political choice that one could either accept or reject. It has instead been imposed on its subjects as a moral system, a moral system increasingly enforced by law. Within this system there are good Whites who welcome racial diversity and bad Whites ("racists") who don't. In that sense multiracialism is an ideological totalitarianism, and there is no point minimizing its present strength. The power that can send police officers to seize a British politician like Nick Griffin, for the speech-crime of criticizing Islam, is real physical power. The power that can drop bombs on the maternity wing of a Serb hospital, in order to cure the inhabitants of their intolerance, is real physical power of an especially savage kind. Multiracialists in Belgium can criminalize a nationalist political party when it becomes too popular for their comfort. In democratic Germany there are more political prisoners in jail today than there were under the Marxist GDR. In America a media-driven machinery of political correctness has successfully stigmatized anyone who dissents from multiracialism's implausible orthodoxies. That, too, is real power, though of a less tangible variety. But despite wielding all this power, multiracialists know that most Whites have not yet embraced their moral system. Any suggestion that there are legitimate alternatives becomes a source of fearful anxiety. Multiracialists try to prevent their opponents from speaking because they believe that most Whites would want to listen, and thus they fear anything, even old operas by a dead heretic, that challenges their totalitarian ideology.

http://library.flawlesslogic.com/wagner2.htm

Some Remarks on "Racism"

I have not yet read Edgar Steele's *Defensive Racism*, but from Michael Polignano's recent review[1] I can see that it distinguishes good from bad "racism." In Steele's terminology the good racism, which he calls "defensive racism," includes opposing affirmative action and practicing self-segregation. "Offensive racism," springing from racial hatred or an aggressive belief in White racial superiority, includes lynching Blacks and shouting racial epithets in your local supermarket. In this usage members of organizations opposing Third World immigration are defensive racists; the killers of James Byrd are offensive racists.

The number of these offensive racists is small, though they are important figures in multiracialism's demonology and play a prominent role in popular culture. (The former, of course, explains the latter.) The number of defensive racists is larger. It is certainly growing, though not as quickly as we would like. Most Whites are potential recruits to the cause of defensive racism, whose central tenet is that people of European descent constitute a group with legitimate interests, which we have a perfect right to defend.

Almost all advocates of pro-White politics agree that a linguistic separation from the label "racism" is necessary. The preference of most White nationalists is to take "racialism" as the name of our core belief system, but for

---

[1] Michael J. Polignano, "Defensible Racism: Edgar Steele's *Defensive Racism*," in *Taking Our Own Side*, ed. Greg Johnson (San Francisco: Counter-Currents Publishing, 2010).

some this sounds like a deceptive euphemism, as though racialists were sloppily attempting, by adding a few letters, to evade the real term, too timid to announce openly what we really are. My own view on this semantic issue is fixed: I will never use "racism" as a serious word, because it isn't.

"Racism" is a propaganda term devised and developed for the purpose of stigmatizing any racial self-assertion by Whites. That has *always* been its purpose. "Racism" has never been anything other than a device of anti-White propaganda. "Racism" and "racist" were not corrupted by politicized usage; they were corrupt to begin with. We should therefore speak of "racism" only when we are describing the propaganda system we hope to defeat. Calling yourself a "racist" or even a "defensive racist" is tantamount to acknowledging both the validity and the permanence of your enemy's greatest propaganda victory.

The French writer Guillaume Faye describes "racism" as a bomb that exploded in the 1960s, but for the English-speaking world noxious weed would be a better metaphor. In American English "racism" began small and obscure during the 1930s, but it spread widely in the decades that followed, eventually growing into a perverse moral system that instructs Whites that the pursuit (or even the mere defense) of their own group interests is a terrible crime.

We should try, as a brief thought experiment, to cast our minds back to the era before the arrival of "racism." If in 1920 someone had claimed that prohibiting non-White immigration into White nations was "racist," no one would have had any idea what he meant, because the label "racism" had not yet come into existence. Without "racism," proponents of multiracial anti-nations would be forced to defend their objectives in the dispassionate language of reasoned discourse, and they would certainly fail, because their objectives are far from reasonable. It is no great challenge to prove that importing fanatical Muslims into Holland or primitive Nigerians into the United States is bad for Whites. Samuel Francis, in an important essay on the origins of "racism," states the matter well:

> "Racism" ... is a term originating on the left, and has been so defined and loaded with meanings the left wants it to have that it cannot now be used by the supporters of white racial consciousness for any constructive purpose. Anyone who uses the term to describe himself or his own views has already allowed himself to be maneuvered onto his opponents' ground and has already lost the debate. He may try to define the word differently, but he will need to spend most of his time explaining that he does not mean by it what everyone else means. As a term useful for communicating ideas that the serious supporters of white racial consciousness wish to communicate, the term is useless, and it was intended by those who developed it that it be useless for that purpose.[2]

National Vanguard (online), January 30, 2005

---

[2] Sam Francis, "The Origins of 'Racism': The Curious Beginnings of a Useless Word," *American Renaissance*, vol. 10, no. 5, May 1999, http://www.amren.com/ar/1999/05/index.html#article1

AMY BIEHL:
A WHITE LIBERAL ON THE DARK CONTINENT

News events and political interpretations of news events rarely coincide exactly. Life is generally messy and complicated, whereas political analysis aims, often legitimately, to simplify life's complexity into a coherent pattern with a convincing political meaning.

Consider, briefly, the case of Wyoming's Matthew Shepard, a central figure in the American Left's ongoing propaganda campaign against the alleged evils of "homophobia." Shepard was HIV-positive on the night he propositioned, in a Laramie bar, two heterosexual men for sex. That inconvenient fact detracts from the political narrative of his martyrdom at the hands of intolerant homophobes, which is why the liberal media, the principal agents of the campaign against "intolerance" and "homophobia," seldom mention it. Anyone who knows about Shepard's HIV-status will also know that he was, in effect if not intention, inviting his prospective sex partners to share his own self-inflicted death sentence. If they had complied with his request for homosexual sex, they could have eventually died from AIDS, just as Shepard himself was destined eventually to die from AIDS, had his killers not ended his life first. An inconvenient fact that doesn't fit the media's political agenda has therefore been excluded from almost all journalistic accounts of the event.

Shepard's murder is, nonetheless, broadly congruent with the political interpretation it has now received, the anti-homophobic narrative into which it has been shaped. Shepard died, clearly, because his murderers disliked homosexuals and visited their distaste for homosexuality upon him; he would not have died if most heterosexual men did not find sexual propositions from homosexuals offensive. He therefore died because of homophobia. If we stand back from our own biases, even those of us who share the traditional distaste ("homophobia") for gay sexual practices must concede that the Left's interpretation of Shepard's murder is reasonable. We could probably see ourselves exploiting the same politically simplified version of the event, without much ethical hesitation, if we held the same political views that its promoters hope to inculcate. An inconvenient fact had to be suppressed in order to make Shepard's murder serve its leftist political purpose, but life rarely provides the same clarity as propaganda.

The death of Amy Biehl is an exception, one of those rare cases where mere recitation of all the facts should be sufficient to demonstrate a convincing political meaning. But in the case of Biehl's murder the political meaning with which her story is now endowed is the exact opposite of what the bare facts would lead any rational, unbiased observer to conclude. Biehl has become a symbolic martyr to the cause of multiracial democracy both in South Africa, where she died at the hands of a savage Black mob, and in the United States, where she had acquired her naive multiracialist ideals, specifically her hopelessly misguided faith in the possibility of democratic self-government by savage Black mobs.

Amy Elizabeth Biehl, by all accounts a talented, intelligent woman, arrived in South Africa in 1993 as an exchange student on a Fulbright Fellowship and was continuing her Ph.D. studies in political science at the mainly Black University of the Western Cape. She left Stanford, where she had received her earlier degrees, for South Africa with anti-racialist political objectives in mind. She wanted to fight apartheid, which she passionately opposed, and accordingly spent much of her time registering Black voters in South Africa's first all-race elections, scheduled for April of 1994, which would hand over political control of the country to its Black majority.

Biehl would have acknowledged, openly and proudly, that she was working against her own race and on behalf of another race, the Black race. That was the principal ideological source of her now celebrated idealism. She wanted to fight White "racism"; she wanted to help its supposed Black victims.

On August 25, 1993, Biehl was driving three Black companions through Cape Town's Guguletu Township. A mob of toyi-toying supporters of the Pan-Africanist Congress (PAC), fresh from a raucous political meeting, attacked her car, pelting it with stones and smashing its windows while shouting "One settler, one bullet," a PAC slogan popular among South African Blacks, "settler" being a synonym for a White South African. Biehl was struck in the head with a brick and, bleeding heavily, dragged from her vehicle. As she tried to flee, stumbling, across the road, she was surrounded by a throng of Blacks who repeatedly kicked, stoned, and stabbed her. The fatal wound, among many, came from a knife, buried to its hilt, that entered under her ribs and ended in her heart.

It is now claimed by her eulogists that Biehl died bravely. But the truth is that she didn't. She died begging for her life. No one can blame her, of course, but the story of Amy's bravery is just a pious lie. She died as most of us would die under similar circumstances—a degrading, abject death, beseeching her tormentors for mercy, but receiving none.

Four of Biehl's assailants, from among the dozen or so who attacked her, were arrested and convicted, but in July of 1998, in the wake of apartheid's demise, they were released from prison, on the ground that the motive for her murder had been political. The killers had believed that her death would help end apartheid, Desmond Tutu's Truth and Reconciliation Commission concluded. She was, as the Commission further observed, simply a representative White in the wrong place at the wrong time. As one of the killers testified: "We were in very high spirits and the White people were oppressive; we had no mercy on the White people. A White person was a White person to our eyes."

Amy's father, demonstrating how thoroughly he shared his daughter's anti-racialist convictions, shook hands with her murderers and encouraged their release. Peter Biehl told reporters: "We hope they will receive the support necessary to live productive lives in a non-violent atmosphere. In fact, we hope the spirits of Amy and of those like her will be a force in their new lives." Two of the freed killers were, however, subsequently accused of rape, a common pastime in the "New South Africa," and have since fled prosecution; Amy's parents selflessly assumed the White man's burden and befriended the other two. Doubtless Amy herself would have befriended her father's killers, had he been killed by a Black mob instead of her. Such is the nature of anti-racialist idealism: It thrives on the most outrageous violations of normal human loyalties.

In itself a single case, like Matt Shepard's or Amy Biehl's, proves nothing, no matter how compelling. At most it only provides a face and a specific life history for a larger factual argument, which should either succeed or fail on the basis of its intrinsic merits and on the weight of evidence its advocates can convincingly adduce, not on the emotions the face and specific life history evoke. But if Amy Biehl's death, taken in isolation from other facts, demonstrates anything, it is surely not the likelihood of successful Black government in post-apartheid South Africa. Not even the most delusional liberal, one would think, could possibly draw that meaning from the brutal racial killing of a defenseless, anti-racialist White woman. Yet that, nevertheless, is the significance her murder, remarkably, has been assigned. The death of Amy Biehl represents, in the eyes of her hagiographers, a meaningful sacrifice to the noble cause of racial harmony and multiracial democracy, now well on their way to realization in the New South Africa. It is a political interpretation that requires, much like anti-racialism itself, an almost supernatural ability to overlook pertinent facts.

"In her death," Peter Biehl now imagines, "Amy created . . . a new consciousness of the depths of human denial and of the raw potential of a free nation." Accordingly the Amy Biehl Foundation has been established to continue what Biehl's parents call "Amy's unfinished legacy": American schoolchildren are indoctrinated in the purported but highly implausible "lesson" of Amy's life — that "a single person can make a difference," just like Amy ostensibly did; musical instruments are distributed to budding Black South African musicians; cosmetics and perfumes are, perhaps quixotically, distributed in Amy's name to needy women in the Black townships and squatter camps; more substantively, training programs for Blacks are funded, in which two of Amy's killers participate, at the moment successfully; a bakery has been established, selling "Amy's Bread — the bread of hope and peace."

EULOGIES FOR SAINT AMY

"She made our aspirations her own and lost her life in the turmoil of our transition as the new South Africa struggled to be born in the dying moments of apartheid." (Nelson Mandela)

"... as she went through her days we saw that she embodied the ideal of making a difference; of living a life with meaning and impact. In truth, the way that Amy lived her life just as much as the way she lost her life gave that life special meaning. She believed that all people have value; that the disadvantaged have special claim on the lives of the more fortunate and that racial justice and racial harmony were ideals worth fighting for and living for and, if need be, dying for." (Secretary of State Madeleine Albright)

"Millions of individuals of all races and backgrounds in the United States and around the world followed Nelson Mandela's example and fought for the abolition of apartheid in the Republic of South Africa, and in this regard, the Congress especially recognizes Amy Elizabeth Biehl, an American student who lost her life in the struggle to free South Africa from racial oppression..." (Senator Carol Moseley-Braun)

"In the township she loved she died for the cause she embraced with heart and soul and so her Spirit lived!... A divine grace creates through agony and pain a profound transfiguration: Weakness to Strength, Fear to Hope, Anger to Joy, Hatred to Love. She will live with us again. " (Internet poet William Davis, author of "Amy Biehl Lives")

The obvious problem with the anti-racialist interpretation of Biehl's martyrdom is, of course, that the wrong people martyred her. That is not merely a small and thus dispensable "inconvenient fact" intruding itself into an otherwise convincing liberal narrative, starring Amy as the bearer of hope and peace for a "New South Africa." It is, rather, central to the event: She died, as a representative White, so that people like her killers could govern people like herself, her fellow Europeans, her racial kinsmen.

Black violence is also central, very tangibly, to the Black-governed South Africa that Biehl worked, in her own modest way, to create. Her death at the hands of a Black mob was not unusual in 1993. Exactly a month earlier PAC terrorists, practicing their own brand of anti-apartheid activism, had massacred congregants in a White church with grenades and rifle fire, killing eleven and wounding fifty-eight, a portent of the even greater violence that majority-rule would soon unleash. The "New South Africa" is, with twenty-seven thousand murders per year, the most dangerous place on earth.

It can also boast of more rapes per capita than any other country; a South African woman is now raped every twenty-six seconds, about forty percent of the victims enduring sadistic gang rapes (or "jackrolling," as its Black practitioners call it). White farmers, in concrete enactments of the venerable ANC slogan "Kill the Boer, kill the farmer," are now regularly tortured and murdered in brutal, often horrifyingly brutal attacks on their isolated rural homes; farming is thus statistically post-apartheid South Africa's most dangerous profession. Carjackings are now so routine that motorists run red lights rather than risk stopping their vehicles, armed robberies likewise so routine that only in exceptional circumstances do the media bother to report them. Suburban Whites now cower at night behind barred windows, which of course do little to protect them from home invasions, and the more affluent are retreating to fortified enclaves, away from exploding crime in South Africa's formerly First World cities.

All of this, along with an accelerating economic collapse, was predictable and was in fact vocally predicted by White defenders of apartheid, who knew what "multiracial democracy" would mean for their people. With average IQs in the low 70s, most sub-Saharan Africans are mentally retarded by European standards and thus incapable of either creating or maintaining an advanced, Western society. Black-governed South Africa is simply descending, gradually but inexorably, to the primitive level of the rest of Black Africa. That's what everyone, including Amy Biehl, should have expected.

Biehl selected South Africa for her benevolent ministrations, rather than Rwanda or Sierra Leone, because she recognized that it was the continent's only successful economy. Her parents report:

> Amy used to tell us that Africa was the "continent of the future." Amy was drawn by the numerous democratic struggles throughout the continent. She knew that these emerging democracies would awaken and transform a sleeping giant. She recognized that—because of its economic sophistication and developed infrastructure—a democratic South Africa could become the dominant player in an African transformation. This realization—coupled with the depth and breadth of human rights abuse—took Amy to South Africa.

Comment should be superfluous. Black Africa has, needless to say, not a single genuine "emerging democracy" and not even a single functioning nation-state. Somehow Amy Biehl, a Ph.D. student in political science, failed to grasp that South Africa's "economic sophistication and developed infrastructure" were products of the Whites who governed it and the Whites who, under apartheid, comprised its citizenry.

In the early 1990s, while White liberal activists, assisted

by their more sanguinary Black colleagues, worked busily for the dispossession of South African Whites from the homeland that their ancestors had built, the economic output of all of sub-Saharan Black Africa, with a population of about six hundred million, was less than Sweden's, population eight million. Then, as now, eighteen of the world's twenty poorest nations were in Black Africa. Then, as now, Black Africa—which under European colonialism had produced ninety-eight percent of its food requirements—was the world's largest recipient of food aid. Then, as now, Black Africa was plagued with endemic hunger, disease, violence and war. Apartheid South Africa, governed by its hated White minority, was the only sub-Saharan exception, the only success story on the entire Dark Continent. But in six short years Black misgovernment has turned South Africa into just another Black failure.

Anti-racialism is more a religious faith than a set of political convictions. Hence the virtual irrelevance of facts in the minds of its most dedicated votaries. White-governed South Africa, like White-governed Rhodesia before it, was always an attractive target for liberal activists, because the very presence of Whites enabled them to ascribe, to their own satisfaction at least, Black poverty and violence to White malevolence. Most deliberately closed their eyes to the fact of Black Africa's manifest failure elsewhere and willed themselves to believe that a Black-governed South Africa would, miraculously, become the continent's sole exception. Although they knew the abundant evidence that indicated otherwise, they chose, in their own anti-racialist version of Orwellian double-think, to allow their knowledge to remain inert, with no effect on their equalitarian beliefs, in order that their ideals could remain uncontaminated by evidence.

Should deracinated liberals receive a moral pass for a

willed failure to notice the utterly obvious? And wasn't the eruption, in a very physical form, of obvious racial realities into a life devoted to delusional anti-racialist activism really the most striking feature of Biehl's brutal murder? The legend of Amy Biehl implausibly claims that her death was a significant sacrifice for a worthy objective. But in simpler and far more convincing terms she was just a naive liberal do-gooder who received, fatally, an unmerited but unsurprising lesson in the real world's indifference to idealistic fantasies.

http://library.flawlesslogic.com/biehl.htm

JANE ELLIOTT &
DIVERSITY TRAINING

COMMISSAR ELLIOTT'S EXPERIMENT

On the day after Martin Luther King, Jr. was murdered in April 1968, Jane Elliott's third graders from the small, all-white town of Riceville, Iowa, came to class confused and upset. They recently had made King their "Hero of the Month," and they couldn't understand why someone would kill him. So Elliott decided to teach her class a daring lesson in the meaning of discrimination. She wanted to show her pupils what discrimination feels like, and what it can do to people.

Elliott divided her class by eye color—those with blue eyes and those with brown. On the first day, the brown-eyed children were told they were smarter, nicer, neater, and better than those with blue eyes. Throughout the day, Elliot praised them and allowed them privileges such as a taking a longer recess and being first in the lunch line. In contrast, the blue-eyed children had to wear collars around their necks, and their behavior and performance were criticized and ridiculed by Elliott. On the second day, the roles were reversed and the brown-eyed children were made to feel inferior while the blue eyes were designated the dominant group. (Excerpted from http://www.pbs.org/)

Jane Elliott's influential training exercise was essentially a form of child abuse put into practice for well over a decade in a small school in rural Iowa. It presupposed that the racial differences that distinguish Blacks from Whites are entirely inconsequential, simply a matter of superficial differences in appearance. She selected eye color as an inconsequential physical feature that illustrated the supposed errors of White "racism" and the suffering of its victims. Just as Whites had historically inflicted terrible suffering on Blacks based merely on the color of their skin, Elliott's White students would experience analogous suffering based merely on the color of their eyes.

Elliott initially stigmatized the blue-eyed White children in her third-grade class as criminally inferior and subjected them to abuse by the brown-eyed White children. Then, in the second stage of her exercise, she reversed the hierarchy, with blue-eyed Whites becoming the preferred group, encouraged to abuse brown-eyed Whites just as they had been abused in the first stage. In other words, both groups of Euro-American children were compelled to become the victims of Elliott's manufactured "racism."

We should emphasize that this dose of educational sadism was administered to young kids in the third grade. Jane Elliott's grand idea was that the White children in her class should be forced to become both racial tormentors and racial victims, and that they should learn how the suffering they experienced as victims had been based on an insignificant physical feature, eye color, over which they had no control. They would experience a small, concentrated sample of what Elliott believed was the near-genocidal oppression that Euro-Americans had imposed on Blacks. The White children were, as far as Elliott was concerned, getting off lightly: They deserved far more punishment for their inherited racial sins than she could possibly inflict.

For this bizarre educational exercise, tormenting powerless children to combat their racial prejudices, Elliott became famous, and in the years that followed she expanded her anti-racialist career, becoming a leading diversity trainer and the subject of a fawning PBS documentary honoring her accomplishments in the holy war against White "racism." Her more recent diversity-education seminars, also celebrated in a television documentary, are just as racially demeaning as the cruel exploit that first won her fame in the 1960s.

Elliott's experiment, like most exercises in diversity training, was nothing less than pedagogical Maoism. Diversity education begins with the belief that Whites as a group are disfigured by a severe racial pathology, which has caused untold suffering to countless numbers of innocent persons of color. Whites acquire this pathology from their parents and from the surrounding Eurocentric society, but by strenuous efforts in reeducation they can be at least partially liberated from it. The psychological and physical welfare of racial minorities demands that this therapeutic liberation occur.

If you're White, there is something profoundly and dangerously wrong with you, even if (like a third-grade kid in an all-White community) you've never been in any position to mistreat minorities. You can hurt Blacks even if you've never met a Black, which was the case for all of Elliott's initial child subjects. That's because the racial assumptions that you have learned from your parents and from the cultural environment that your White forefathers created themselves constitute an insidious assault on racial minorities, spawning a pervasive and destructive "racism" that must be ameliorated, though it can never be entirely eradicated, by repeated immersion in programs of racial reeducation. Diversity trainers are not, by the way, afraid of this word "reeducation," despite its bloodstained history in the reeducational campaigns of Marxist killers from Stalin to Pol Pot.

Most *National Vanguard* readers will, of course, have detected the massive fallacy inherent in Elliott's experiment. It is clearly untrue that the racial differences between Blacks and Whites are as inconsequential as the difference between blue and brown eyes. Blacks are, for example, statistically more violent than Whites and score lower in measured intelligence, and those non-debatable facts would remain true even if, as Elliott and her ilk wrongly believe, race is an artificial social construction rather than a hard genetic reality.

There is, however, a small but significant truth in the common leftist claim that race is a social construction, a truth from which any non-racialist Whites reading this can learn an important lesson.

Elliott, to her credit, is principled in her evil. In her current diversity seminars no White — man or woman, liberal or conservative, firefighter or bank president, recent European immigrant or old-stock Anglo-Saxon — escapes racial vilification. Elliott attacks Whites as Whites. All of us have been infected with what she calls the "live virus of racism." Even if you are a naively raceless White, for the growing diversity industry you remain a mentally diseased enemy whose thoughts and unconscious attitudes must be unlearned or restructured. In that respect your racial identity as a Euro-American is indeed a construction produced by the political and quasi-therapeutic forces arrayed against you, forces that will undoubtedly gain greater strength as non-White demographics expand. You may be an inveterate celebrator of diversity and a supporter of open-borders immigration and compensatory discrimination, but you are still criminally White in the eyes of diversity trainers. Like affirmative action, diversity training objectively defines you as White regardless of your own subjective self-identification. You become, to borrow a term from multiculturalism's academic jargon, a member of a "racialized population," assigned to a fixed racial category whether you like it or not.

The lesson: White nationalism is rational self-defense. If you are attacked as a member of a group, then you must defend your group in order to defend yourself.

http://library.flawlesslogic.com/elliott.htm

www.ingramcontent.com/pod-product-compliance
Lightning Source LLC
Chambersburg PA
CBHW031629160426
43196CB00006B/336